提高篇
我的英语日记书

主编：清 瑶
编委：宝洛尔

超有趣的英语日记书！

北京理工大学出版社
BEIJING INSTITUTE OF TECHNOLOGY PRESS

版权专有　侵权必究

图书在版编目（CIP）数据

我的英语日记书. 提高篇 / 清瑶主编. — 北京：北京理工大学出版社，2019.9

ISBN 978-7-5682-7556-9

Ⅰ. ①我… Ⅱ. ①清… Ⅲ. ①英语 – 日记 – 写作 – 小学 – 教学参考资料 Ⅳ. ① G624.313

中国版本图书馆 CIP 数据核字（2019）第 197422 号

出版发行 / 北京理工大学出版社有限责任公司
社　　址 / 北京市海淀区中关村南大街 5 号
邮　　编 / 100081
电　　话 /（010）68914775（总编室）
　　　　　（010）82562903（教材售后服务热线）
　　　　　（010）68948351（其他图书服务热线）
网　　址 / http://www.bitpress.com.cn
经　　销 / 全国各地新华书店
印　　刷 / 汇昌印刷（天津）有限公司
开　　本 / 710 毫米 × 1000 毫米　1/16
印　　张 / 10
字　　数 / 112 千字
版　　次 / 2019 年 9 月第 1 版　2019 年 9 月第 1 次印刷
定　　价 / 32.80 元

责任编辑 / 赵兰辉
文案编辑 / 李文文
责任校对 / 周瑞红
责任印制 / 施胜娟

图书出现印装质量问题，请拨打售后服务热线，本社负责调换

前 言

《英语课程标准》对基础教育阶段听、说、读、写四个技能提出了九个级别的目标要求,其中在语言技能(听说读写)二级"写"的目标描述中明确要求:"小学生能模仿范例写句子;能写出简单的问候语;能根据要求为图片、实物等写出简短的标题或描述;能基本正确地使用大小写字母和标点符号。"

英语写作教学是小学英语教学中非常重要的部分,贯穿整个教学过程。写作教学对帮助学生了解英语思维的方式,养成运用英语思维进行思考的习惯,提高学生综合运用语言知识的能力大有益处。

本套丛书旨在为初学英语的小学生在英语写作方面提供一些指导和帮助。本书分为5个单元,每个单元一个话题,话题围绕小学生的日常生活展开。通过"好词妙妙屋—语法小贴士—语法大擂台—日记导图秀—参考范文—词汇加油站"等栏目,由浅入深、循序渐进地进

行训练，帮助学生正确地使用词汇，锻炼学生组织句子的能力。每篇日记都是一个小故事，并配上有趣的图片，帮助小学生理解日记内容，图文并茂，趣味盎然。"日记导图秀"栏目设置了提示性问题，能有效地帮助学生写出相应话题的段落；"语法小贴士"栏目为小学生提供相应的语法辅导，帮助学生们运用正确的句式进行写作训练。

　　我们衷心地希望本套丛书能够帮助小学生更好地掌握英语写作的方法，使学生们不断提高英语成绩。本套丛书必然还存在很多需要改进之处，恳请读者批评指正，更望专家不吝赐教。

目录 Contents

Unit 1 About Me

1. Myself — 002
2. My Parents — 008
3. My Dream — 013
4. My Favorite Season — 019
5. I Have a Computer — 025

Unit 2 Travel and Places

6. Travel Plan — 032
7. The Great Wall — 038
8. My Hometown — 044
9. My School — 050
10. Visiting Mount Tai — 055

Unit 3 A Colorful Life

11. A Day in the Zoo — 062
12. My Birthday Party — 068
13. On Duty — 073
14. Sports Meeting — 079
15. My First Day at School — 085

目录 Contents

Unit 4
Beautiful Nature

16. The River in My Hometown 092
17. My Favorite Animal 098
18. Winter Is Coming! 104
19. A Clever Crow 109
20. How to Protect the Environment 114

Unit 5
Future Life and Fantasies

21. My Future House 120
22. My Future Job 125
23. The Future Cars 130
24. If I Had the Wings 136
25. I Had a Dream 142

Unit 1
About Me

1. Myself

June 3rd   Monday   Sunny

Hello, everyone! I'm Dobby from Australia. Now I live and study in Shanghai.

I came to China four years ago. At that time, I couldn't speak Chinese. I had no friends to play with. But now, I can speak Chinese well. And I have many friends. They teach me Chinese and I teach them English. We get along very well with each other.

I love living in China!

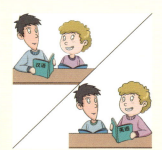

UNIT 1 About Me

好词妙妙屋

myself 我自己   ago 以前   speak 说

four years ago 4年前   at that time 那时
get along well with 与……相处得很好   each other 互相

参考译文

6月3日　　　　　　星期一　　　　　　晴

　　大家好！我叫多比，来自澳大利亚。现在我在上海居住和学习。

　　我四年前来到了中国。那时，我不会说中文，也没有朋友一起玩。但是现在，我中文说得很好，也交了很多朋友。他们教我说中文，我教他们说英语。我们相处得非常好。

　　我非常喜欢在中国生活。

语法小贴士

　　在中文里，当我们要表达过去或现在的事情时，我们会在句子里添加表示过去时间或现在时间的词。但是在英语中，我们除了要添加表示时间的词外，还要对动词做相应的处理。这就需要用到英语中的时态了。

　　英语中主要有八大时态，在小学阶段，我们只学习四种，分别是：一般现在时、一般过去时、一般将来时和现在进行时。今天我们就来简单地了解一下英语的时态。

1. 一般现在时表示现在发生的事情或存在的状态，可以表示习惯，和 often, usually 等频度副词连用。

   There are five people in my family. 我家有五口人。

   The sun rises from the east. 太阳从东方升起。

   I usually go to school at half past seven. 我通常七点半去上学。

2. 一般过去时表示过去经常或偶然发生的动作，或存在的状态。

   When did you start to go to school? 你什么时候开始去上学的？

   My father often went to work by bus.
   我爸爸以前经常坐公交车去上班。

   There used to be a cinema in our city. 我们市过去有一家电影院。

3. 一般将来时表示将来某个时间要发生的动作、事情，或存在的状态。

   I will go to visit the Great Wall this summer holiday.
   我今年暑假要去游览长城。

   There is going to be a Disney Park in our city.
   我们市将要有一座迪士尼公园。

4. 现在进行时表示正在进行或发生的动作。

   It is raining outside. 外面正在下雨。

   I am reading a book. 我正在看书。

About Me

UNIT 1

语法大擂台

读句子，根据图片信息完成句子。

1. I often _____ at 6:00 in the morning.

2. I will go to the _____ this afternoon.

3. My father is _____ for me.

4. Xiao Ming _____ a tiger yesterday.

5. My mother _____ in the kitchen.

6. There will be a _____ match tomorrow.

7. Dobby wanted to _____ the Great Wall.

8. I _____ at half past nine every evening.

我的英语日记书 提高篇

日记导图秀

小朋友，请你模仿上面的日记，写一篇关于自己的日记吧！

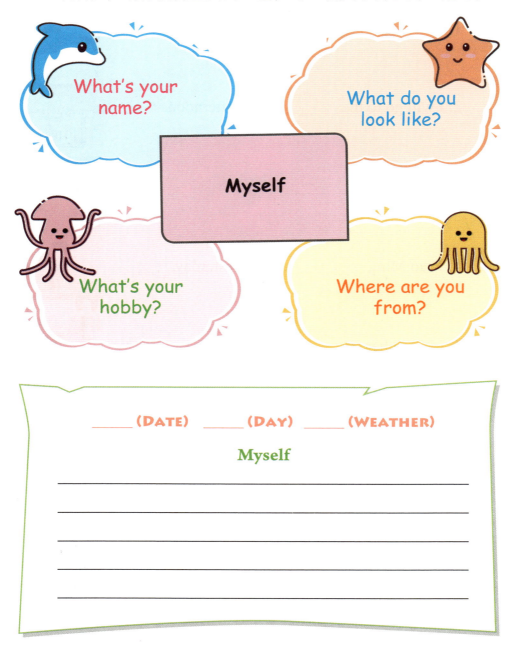

_____(DATE) _____(DAY) _____(WEATHER)

Myself

_____
_____
_____
_____
_____

Unit 1 About Me

参考范文

June 22nd   Saturday   Sunny

Myself

Hello, everyone! I'm Xiao Ming. I come from Shanghai, China.

I'm tall and thin. When I was very young, I was very sick. But now I'm strong. I love sports very much. I can play basketball, football and tennis. In fact, I'm the captain in our school basketball team.

This is me! Do you like me?

词汇加油站

> 描写自己还可以用：

I used to be very shy. 我过去很害羞。

I don't like talking too much. 我不太喜欢说话。

I'm very kind and helpful. 我很善良，而且乐于助人。

I have big eyes and long hair. 我眼睛大，头发长。

2. My Parents

April 8th   **Sunday**   **Sunny**

    My parents are very busy every day. My father is a taxi driver. He is a particular driver in Shanghai, because he is the only foreigner to drive a taxi. He works from 7:00 in the morning to 9:00 in the evening. My mother is a nurse. She is busier than my father. Sometimes, she works in the hospital for several days.

    My parents are busy, but they love me very much. When they have free time, they will take me out. I love them, too.

About Me
UNIT 1

好词妙妙屋

busy 忙碌的　　　　particular 特殊的　　　　because 因为
only 唯一的　　　　foreigner 外国人　　　　sometimes 有时

every day 每天　　　　　　taxi driver 出租车司机
be busier than 比……忙　　free time 休闲时间

参考译文

4月8日　　　　　　星期日　　　　　　晴

　　我的爸爸妈妈每天都非常忙。我的爸爸是上海的一位出租车司机。他是一位特别的司机，因为他是唯一开出租车的外国人。他每天从早上7点工作到晚上9点。我的妈妈是一名护士，她比爸爸还要忙，有时她会在医院里连续工作好几天。

　　虽然爸爸妈妈很忙，但是他们很爱我。当他们休息时，他们就会带我出去。我也非常爱他们。

语法小贴士

　　当我们用英语描述现在发生的事或者介绍一件事、一件物品时，我们就要用到一般现在时。那么一般现在时都有哪些特点呢？我们今天就来学习一下。

人称与数

1. 当主语是第一人称和第二人称时,动词用原形。如:

   I live in Shanghai. 我住在上海。

   You speak English very well. 你英语说得非常好。

2. 当主语是第三人称时,动词要变成第三人称单数形式。如:

   My father drives a taxi. 我爸爸开出租车。

   My mother works in a hospital. 我妈妈在医院工作。

第三人称单数变化规则

和名词变复数一样,动词变第三人称单数也有其变化规则:

① 通常情况是在词尾加 -s。如:

   work—works; buy—buys; speak—speaks

② 以 s, x, sh, ch 结尾的单词,在词尾加 -es。如:

   watch—watches; wash—washes

③ 以 y 结尾的单词中,如果 y 前面的是元音字母,在词尾直接加 -s;如果 y 前面的是辅音字母,就需要把 y 变成 i,再加 -es。如:

   play—plays; study—studies

④ 有两个特殊的单词需要特别记忆。

   do—does; have—has

语法大擂台

请写出下列动词的第三人称单数形式。

1. drink _____   2. go _____   3. stay _____
4. make _____   5. look _____   6. pass _____
7. carry _____   8. come _____   9. plant _____
10. brush _____   11. do _____   12. have _____

About Me

UNIT 1

日记导图秀

小朋友，你爸爸妈妈在做什么工作？请你模仿上面的日记，自己写一篇关于他们的日记吧！

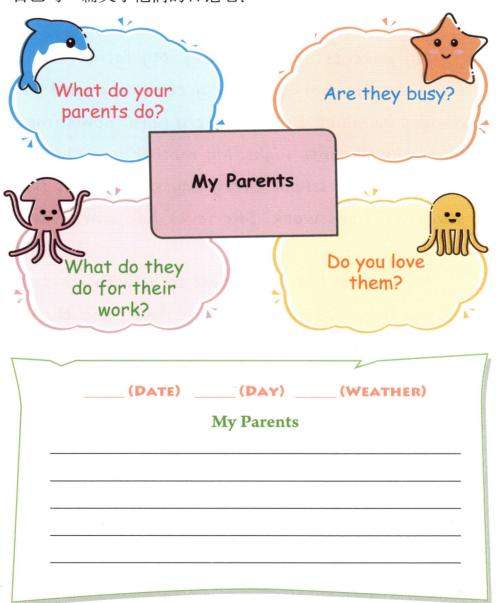

| January 15th | Tuesday | Snowy |

My Parents

My parents are very busy. My father is an engineer. He works in a big company, and he designs buildings. He works very hard. Sometimes he works late into night. My mother is a Chinese teacher in our school. Every day she corrects the students' homework. She loves her work very much.

My parents have little time to be with me, but I know they love me very much. And I love them, too.

> **描写职业的名词还有：**

worker 工人　　doctor 医生　　police 警察

chef 厨师　　driver 司机　　pilot 飞行员

lawyer 律师　　tour guide 导游

About Me

🎧 3. My Dream

| May 26th | Sunday | Rainy |

   Everyone has his dream, and my dream is to be a pilot.

   When I was very young and saw the plane over my head, I was very excited. I always dream to drive a plane flying in the sky. I also want to drive a plane to Australia myself.

   From now on, I must study hard, and do more exercises to make me strong.

好词妙妙屋

dream 理想　　　　pilot 飞行员　　　　young 年轻的；幼小的
excited 兴奋的　　　sky 天空　　　　　strong 强壮的

My dream is to be a(n)... 我的梦想是成为……
from now on 从今以后　　　study hard 努力学习

参考译文

5月26日　　　　　　星期日　　　　　　雨

　　每个人都有自己的梦想。我的梦想是成为一名飞行员。

　　在我很小的时候，当我看见飞机飞过头顶时，我非常兴奋。我总是梦想着能驾驶飞机飞翔在蓝天上。我也想自己驾驶飞机去澳大利亚。

　　从今以后，我必须要努力学习，多做运动，使我的身体更强壮。

语法小贴士

　　我们在说表示一般现在时的句子时，会经常说"I get up at 6:30." "She visits the library every week."那么，小朋友们，你们了解一般现在时的构成吗？你们会用一般现在时表达想要说的话吗？如果不会，不要紧，就跟着我们进入今天的课堂吧！

UNIT 1 About Me

1. 含有 be 动词的一般现在时

构成：主语 + am/is/are + 其他

I am a student. 我是一名学生。

The boy under the tree is my friend. 树下的那个男孩是我的朋友。

You are my best friend. 你是我最好的朋友。

They are good teachers. 他们是好老师。

变一般疑问句时，将 be 动词放到主语之前，如果主语是第一人称，变疑问句时要将第一人称变为第二人称。如：

I am a student. 我是一名学生。

→ Are you a student? 你是一名学生吗？

The boy under the tree is my friend. 树下的那个男孩是我的朋友。

→ Is the boy under the tree your friend?

树下的那个男孩是你的朋友吗？

They are good teachers. 他们是好老师。

→ Are they good teachers? 他们是好老师吗？

2. 含有情态动词的一般现在时

构成：主语 + 情态动词 + 动词原形 + 其他

I can swim. 我会游泳。

She should go to the park. 她应该去公园。

变一般疑问句时，将情态动词放到主语之前，如果主语是第一人称，变疑问句时要将第一人称变为第二人称。如：

I can swim. 我会游泳。

→ Can you swim? 你会游泳吗？

She should go to the park. 她应该去公园。

→ Should she go to the park? 她应该去公园吗？

3. 实义动词的一般现在时

构成：主语 + 动词原形 / 第三人称单数形式 + 其他

I go to school from Monday to Friday. 我星期一到星期五去上学。

Her mother works in a school. 她妈妈在一所学校工作。

变一般疑问句时，要借助于助动词 do 的适当形式，将其放到主语之前，其余部分按照陈述句语序放在 do 的后边。如果主语是第一人称，变疑问句时要将第一人称变为第二人称。如：

I go to school from Monday to Friday. 我星期一到星期五去上学。

→ Do you go to school from Monday to Friday?

你星期一到星期五去上学吗？

Her mother works in a school. 她妈妈在一所学校工作。

→ Does her mother work in a school? 她妈妈在一所学校工作吗？

语法大擂台

读句子，用所给动词的适当形式填空。

1. I _____ (buy) a present for my mother.

2. She can _____ (play) the piano very well.

3. My father _____ (work) in a company.

4. Can you _____ (speak) Chinese?

5. _____ you _____ (go) to school every day?

6. _____ your mother _____ (like) cooking?

About Me

UNIT 1

日记导图秀

小朋友，你的梦想是什么？快和大家描述一下吧！

_____ (DATE)　_____ (DAY)　_____ (WEATHER)

My Dream

_____

_____

_____

_____

_____

参考范文

March 3rd　　　Saturday　　　Windy

My Dream

Everyone has his dream, and my dream is to be an inventor.

I want to invent a robot. I hope it can help my parents do their jobs. It can help my father control the computer to design buildings. It can also help my mother correct the students' homework. Thus, they can have enough free time to relax.

From now on, I must study hard, and read more books about science.

词汇加油站

> 描写梦想你还可能用到：

I have a dream. 我有一个梦想。

I dream to be... 我梦想成为……

I want to be... because I... 我想成为……，因为……

I dream to have wings. 我梦想有一双翅膀。

About Me

UNIT 1

4. My Favorite Season

| June 27th | Thursday | Sunny |

There are four seasons in a year, and I like autumn best.

Autumn is the season for harvest. Farmers are busy getting in crops and fruits. Autumn is the best time to travel. When autumn comes, all leaves turn yellow gradually, and everywhere becomes golden. That's so beautiful!

好词妙妙屋

season 季节　　　　　　harvest 收获　　　　　　crop 庄稼
gradually 渐渐地　　　　golden 金黄色的

I like... best 我最喜欢……　　　be busy doing 忙着做
get in 收割
It is the best time to... 这是做……的最好时间

参考译文

6月27日　　　　　星期四　　　　　　　晴

　　一年有四季，我最喜欢的是秋天。
　　秋天是收获的季节。农民们忙着收割庄稼、采摘水果。秋天是出游的最佳时间。秋天来临时，树叶渐渐变黄了，到处都是金黄色的，漂亮极了！

语法小贴士

　　我们已经学习了一般现在时的构成和句式变化了，那么小朋友们，你们知道一般现在时的用法吗？知道什么时候用一般现在时吗？知道一般现在时表达的含义吗？今天我们将带大家探索一下其中的奥秘！

UNIT 1 About Me

1. **通常表示人物或事物的特征和状态。如：**

   The sky is blue. 天空是蓝色的。

   I like swimming. 我喜欢游泳。

2. **表示经常性或习惯性动作，常与 often, usually, always, sometimes 等频度副词连用。如：**

   I often get up at half past six. 我经常6点半起床。

   My father always drives to work. 我爸爸总是开车去上班。

3. **表示客观事实和普遍真理。如：**

   The sun rises in the east. 太阳从东方升起。

   The earth travels around the sun. 地球绕着太阳转。

4. **与一般现在时连用的时间状语通常包含：**

   every day/week/month, in the morning/afternoon/evening, once a week, often, usually, sometimes 等。

   I go to swim once a week. 我每周游泳一次。

   I read English every day. 我每天都读英语。

语法大擂台

根据图片及所给单词提示写句子。

1. Dobby and Amy   grapes   water

   _____

2. Fangfang   swim   in the pool

   _____

3. we   picnic   in the park
   _____

4. a boy   football   under a tree
   _____

5. Dobby and his friend   plant   trees
   _____

日记导图秀

小朋友，你最喜欢哪个季节？为什么？在这个季节你可以做什么？请你模仿上面的日记描述一下吧！

UNIT 1 About Me

_____ (DATE) _____ (DAY) _____ (WEATHER)

My Favorite Season

_____
_____
_____
_____
_____

| July 12th | Monday | Rainy |

My Favorite Season

There are four seasons in a year. And my favorite season is summer.

In summer, it is very hot, and the days are longer. For me, there is summer holiday, so I can go to the seaside. I like swimming and I can go swimming in the sea. Besides, I don't go to school in summer holiday. I can play basketball with my friends.

What's your favorite season?

词汇加油站

> **描写最喜欢的季节还可能用到:**

We have four seasons—spring, summer, autumn and winter.
我们有四季——春、夏、秋、冬。

In spring/summer/autumn/winter, I can...
在春天/夏天/秋天/冬天,我可以……

The weather in spring/summer/autumn/winter is...
在春天/夏天/秋天/冬天,天气……

When spring/summer/autumn/winter comes, the trees/flowers/grass...
当春天/夏天/秋天/冬天来临时,树/花/草……

About Me

UNIT 1

5. I Have a Computer

September 15th　　　Sunday　　　Sunny

　　I have a computer. It is my birthday present.
　　It helps me a lot. When I meet some difficult problems, I will search it for answers. I also get lots of international news from the Internet. Besides, I can make friends with people all over the world. I can also play games with my friends during the free time.
　　The computer makes my life colorful. I like it very much.

好词妙妙屋

computer 电脑，计算机　　difficult 困难的　　search 搜索
Internet 网络　　　　　　　besides 此外　　　　colorful 丰富多彩的

---

birthday present 生日礼物　　　　difficult problem 难题
international news 国际新闻　　　make friends with 与……交朋友
all over the world 全世界　　　　free time 空闲时间

参考译文

9月15日　　　　　　星期日　　　　　　晴

　　我有一台电脑，那是我的生日礼物。

　　它帮了我很多。当我遇到难题的时候，我会上网搜索答案。我还能从网络上了解很多国际新闻。此外，我可以和世界各地的人交朋友。我也可以在空闲时间和我的朋友们一起玩游戏。

　　电脑使我的生活变得多姿多彩。我非常喜欢这台电脑。

语法小贴士

　　我们已经知道，表达现在的状态或性质要用一般现在时，那么我们要如何表达过去发生的事呢？还能用一般现在时吗？答案显然是否定的。表达过去发生的事要用一般过去时，今天我们就走进一般过去时的乐园吧！

About Me

UNIT 1

动词过去式的形式：

I **had** eggs, bread and milk for breakfast this morning.
我今天早餐吃了鸡蛋、面包和牛奶。

I **learned** to ride a bike yesterday. 我昨天学会骑自行车了。

I **visited** Beijing last summer holiday. 去年暑假，我游览了北京。

My mother **worked** in a school several years ago.
我妈妈几年前在一所学校工作。

我们发现：表达一般过去时，动词要用过去式形式。

动词过去式的变化规则：

1. 大多数动词后可直接加 -ed，如果以 e 结尾，直接加 -d。如：

   visit—visited 参观　　　　move—moved 搬迁

2. 以"辅音 + 单个元音 + 辅音"结尾的单词，双写尾字母，再加 -ed。如：

   stop—stopped 停止　　　　plan—planned 计划

3. 以"辅音字母 +y"结尾的单词，变 y 为 i，再加 -ed。如：

   carry—carried 携带　　　　worry—worried 担心

语法大擂台

读单词，写出下列动词的过去式。

1. live _____   2. watch _____   3. open _____

4. study _____   5. love _____   6. try _____

7. cry _____   8. stop _____   9. plan _____

我的英语日记书 提高篇

日记导图秀

小朋友,你有没有很特别的物品?它在生活和学习中能帮到你吗?请你模仿上面的日记描写一下吧!

_____(Date) _____(Day) _____(Weather)

I Have a(n)_____

_____
_____
_____
_____
_____

UNIT 1 About Me

参考范文

May 11th   Sunday   Sunny

I Have a Pet Dog

I have a pet dog. Its name is Lucky. My grandpa gave it to me as a birthday present.

Lucky is a white dog. It can do many things. On weekdays, it often awakes me to get up. So I'm never late for school. Lucky is very clever. It can count the numbers. And it can help me do shopping. Every week, I give it a bath to keep it clean.

I like it very much.

词汇加油站

> **在家中我可能还会有：**

a pet cat 一只宠物猫
a basketball/football 一个篮球 / 足球
a story book 一本故事书
a toy car 一辆玩具汽车

> **描述一个物品时还会用到：**

My mother gave it to me on my birthday.
我妈妈在我生日时送我的。
It is very... 它很……
It looks like... 它看起来像……

Unit 2
Travel and Places

6. Travel Plan

June 23rd **Sunday** **Sunny**

Summer holiday is coming. My family wants to go to Beijing. My mother asks me to make a plan.

We will go there by train, because it is fast and we can watch the scenery on the way. We will go to visit the Great Wall, the Palace Museum and the Summer Palace. Besides, we will also watch the flag-raising ceremony.

I hope we will have a good time!

Travel and Places

UNIT 2

好词妙妙屋

fast 快的　　　　　　scenery 景色　　　　　　besides 此外

ask sb. to do... 让某人做……　　　make a plan 制订计划
by train 乘火车　　　　　　　　　on the way 在路上
the flag-raising ceremony 升旗仪式　　have a good time 玩得开心

参考译文

6月23日　　　　　星期日　　　　　　晴

暑假就要到来了。我们一家准备去北京旅游。妈妈让我制订一个旅行计划。

我们准备乘火车去，因为火车很快，并且我们也可以欣赏沿途的风景。我们要去爬长城，参观故宫博物院，游览颐和园。此外，我们还要去观看升旗仪式。

我希望我们能玩得开心！

语法小贴士

我们了解了表达过去发生的事要用一般过去时，也知道了动词过去式的变化规则，但是凡事都有特例。总有那么一些调皮的动词不走寻常路线，它们的过去式不按常规变化，我们特意归纳了几种常见的变化规律。小朋友，一定要记牢哦！

1. **过去式和原形同形。** 如：
   cut—cut 切割　　　put—put 放下　　　let—let 让

2. **将字母 i 改为 a。** 如：
   drink—drank 喝　　sit—sat 坐　　　　sing—sang 唱歌
   swim—swam 游泳　begin—began 开始　give—gave 给

3. **含有 ee 的单词，去掉一个字母 e，词尾加 t；或者，变 ee 为 e。** 如：
   keep—kept 保持　　sleep—slept 睡觉　feel—felt 感觉
   meet—met 遇见　　feed—fed 喂　　　bleed—bled 流血

4. **以 -eep 结尾，改为 -ept。** 如：
   sleep—slept 睡觉　sweep—swept 打扫　keep—kept 保持

5. **以 d 结尾的单词，变 d 为 t。** 如：
   spend—spent 花费；度过　　　　　　build—built 建筑
   lend—lent 借　　　　send—sent 送

6. **"骑马""开车""写字"，把 i 变 o。**
   ride—rode 骑马　　drive—drove 开车　write—wrote 写字

7. **ow/aw 改为 ew。** 如：
   know—knew 知道　grow—grew 生长　draw—drew 画

8. **用 ought/aught 替换。** 如：
   buy—bought 买　　bring—brought 带来　teach—taught 教

9. **另外还有一些单词的过去式需要特别记忆。** 如：
   have—had 拥有　　make—made 制作　take—took 带走
   eat—ate 吃　　　　get—got 获得　　　go—went 去
   leave—left 离开　　run—ran 跑　　　　see—saw 看见
   stand—stood 站立　tell—told 告诉　　wear—wore 穿

Travel and Places

语法大擂台

写出下列动词的过去式，并与相对应的图片连线。

1. swim _____   A

2. sing _____   B

3. eat _____   C

4. fly _____   D

5. fall _____   E

6. drink _____   F

7. run _____   G

8. ride _____   H

9. sweep _____   I

10. draw ____   J

日记导图秀

小朋友，你假期计划出去游玩吗？请根据上面的日记制订一份假期出游计划吧！

- Where will you go?
- How will you go there?
- Who will go with you?
- What will you do there?

Travel Plan

_____ (DATE) _____ (DAY) _____ (WEATHER)

Travel Plan

_____
_____
_____
_____
_____

Unit 2 Travel and Places

参考范文

January 14th　　　Thursday　　　Sunny

Travel Plan

This winter holiday, our family will have a trip. We will go to Australia, because it is very warm in January.

My father likes tennis very much, and he wants to watch the Australian Open. We will visit Sydney Opera House and swim in the sea. Besides, we will see koalas, kangaroos and ostriches. I think they are very cute.

I hope we will have a great trip!

词汇加油站

> 描写旅行还可能用到：

We go there by bus/train/ship/plane.
我们乘公共汽车 / 火车 / 轮船 / 飞机去。
We would like to do... 我们想要做……
On one hand,... on the other hand,...
一方面，……另一方面，……
We should book the tickets and hotel before starting off.
在出发前，我们应该订好车票和旅店。

7. The Great Wall

August 5th   Monday   Sunny

The Great Wall is one of ancient China's most famous buildings. It has a history of more than 2,000 years. It is wide enough for six horses to walk side by side. In the past, the Great Wall was built for fighting against enemies. Now it is one of the most important tourist spots in China. Every year, thousands of people all over the world visit it.

Travel and Places

UNIT 2

好词妙妙屋

ancient 古代的　　　history 历史　　　wide 宽的

side by side 并排　　　fight against 对抗
tourist spot 旅游景点　　thousands of 成千上万的

参考译文

8月5日　　　　星期一　　　　晴

长城是中国古代最著名的建筑之一,它拥有两千多年的历史。它的城墙非常宽,可以允许六匹马并排行走。在过去,长城被用来对抗敌人。现在它是中国最重要的旅游景点之一,每年都有成千上万来自世界各地的游客前往参观。

语法小贴士

我们知道,表达过去发生的动作或事情用动词过去式,我们也掌握了大部分动词过去式的变化规则。那么,小朋友们,你们现在能用动词过去式组句子吗?今天我们就来看一看如何将动词过去式放到句子里。

一般过去时的构成

主语 + 动词过去式 + 其他成分

I went to Beijing last winter. 去年冬天我去了北京。

My mother was a nurse 10 years ago. 我妈妈十年前是一名护士。

一般过去时的用法

1. 表示过去某个时间发生的事情或存在的状态。

   Yesterday I went home at 5 in the afternoon.
   我昨天下午 5 点回家了。

   I was five years old 5 years ago. 五年前我五岁。

2. 表示过去经常或反复发生的动作，常和 often, always 等频度副词连用。

   His father often went to work by bus last year.
   他爸爸去年经常乘公交车去上班。

   My grandpa always helped others when he was young.
   我爷爷年轻时总是帮助别人。

3. 经常与一般过去时连用的时间状语有：last year/month/week, in + 过去时间, yesterday, ago 等。

   Beijing Olympic Games were held in 2008.
   北京奥运会在 2008 年举办。

   It rained heavily yesterday morning. 昨天上午雨下得很大。

一般过去时的疑问句形式

1. 当句子中含有 be 动词或情态动词时，直接将 be 动词或情态动词提前。若主语是第一人称，要改为第二人称。

   I was five years old 5 years ago. 五年前我五岁。

   → Were you five years old 5 years ago? 五岁前你五岁吗？

   She could swim very well. 她以前游泳非常棒。

   → Could she swim very well? 她以前游泳游得非常棒吗？

Travel and Places

UNIT 2

2. 当句子中的谓语是实义动词时，要借助于助动词 did。若主语是第一人称，要改为第二人称。

I went to swim last weekend. 我上周末去游泳了。

→ Did you go to swim last weekend? 你上周末去游泳了没？

语法大擂台

根据图片，补全句子。

1. Yesterday I _____ to school.

2. Last weekend, I _____ the floor.

3. I _____ at 6 this morning.

4. Last Spring, we _____ trees on the hill.

5. I _____ in the sea last summer holiday.

6. We _____ the Palace Museum yesterday.

7. I _____ a football match last weekend.

8. I _____ shopping yesterday afternoon.

我的英语日记书 提高篇

日记导图秀

小朋友，你旅游时对哪个景点印象最深刻？请你模仿上面的日记描述一下吧！

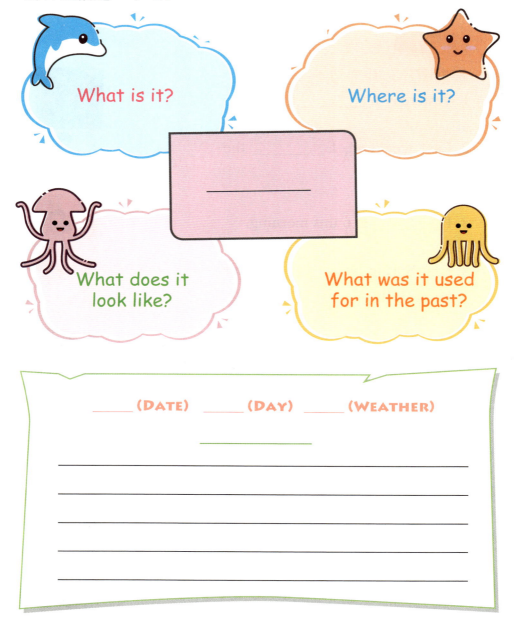

_____ (Date) _____ (Day) _____ (Weather)

Travel and Places

UNIT 2

参考范文

April 21st　　　Sunday　　　Sunny

The West Lake

The West Lake is located in Hangzhou, the capital city of Zhejiang Province. It is not only famous in Hangzhou, but also in the world. It is called the Paradise on the earth.

The best time to visit it is May. At that time, all the trees turn green, and the grass comes out. There are all kinds of flowers around the lake. It is very beautiful. You can also go boating on the lake. It's so wonderful!

词汇加油站

> 介绍景点时还可能用到：

It lies in/is located in... 它位于……

It has a history of... 它拥有……的历史。

It is one of the greatest buildings in...
它是……最伟大的建筑之一。

It attracts thousands of visitors.
它吸引了成千上万的游客。

8. My Hometown

May 8th   **Tuesday**   **Sunny**

My hometown is in Sydney. I think it is the most beautiful city in Australia.

The warmest month in Sydney is January, and the coldest is July. If you want to travel to Sydney, you'd better choose January. You can see many rare animals in Sydney, such as kangaroos and koalas. If you are visiting Sydney, you must try some seafood. They are very delicious.

Travel and Places

UNIT 2

好词妙妙屋

beautiful 美丽的　　warm 温暖的　　month 月份
cold 寒冷的　　　　choose 选择　　kangaroo 袋鼠
koala 考拉　　　　　seafood 海鲜　　delicious 美味的

You'd better do... 你最好做……
rare animal 珍稀动物　　　　such as 例如

参考译文

5月8日　　　　　　星期二　　　　　　晴

　　我的家乡在悉尼，我认为它是澳大利亚最美丽的城市。悉尼最温暖的月份是一月，最冷的是七月。如果你想来悉尼旅游的话，你最好选择一月。悉尼有很多珍稀动物，例如袋鼠和考拉。如果你正在悉尼游玩，你一定要尝一下海鲜，这里的海鲜非常好吃。

语法小贴士

　　在生活中，我们经常听到"我将来要成为一名飞行员。""我将来要出国学习。""我明天要去图书馆。"这些都表达了将来发生的事。那么，小朋友们，你们知道如何用英语来表达将来发生的事吗？今天我们将带大家走进未来的世界！

一般将来时的构成

1. be going to + 动词原形，be 可以用 am, is 和 are。

I am going to visit the Great Wall next week. 我下周要去游览长城。

They are going to have a PE class in the afternoon.
他们下午有一节体育课。

My mother is going to make a cake for my birthday.
我妈妈要为我做一个生日蛋糕。

2. will + 动词原形，没有人称变化，可以和 be going to 互换。

I will visit the Great Wall next week. 我下周要去游览长城。

They will have a PE class in the afternoon. 他们下午有一节体育课。

My mother will make a cake for my birthday.
我妈妈要为我做一个生日蛋糕。

一般将来时的变化

1. 含有 be going to 的一般将来时的变化

（1）变否定句时，直接在 be 动词后加 not。

There is going to be a movie this evening. 今天晚上将有一场电影。

→ There is not going to be a movie this evening.
今天晚上不会放映电影。

（2）变一般疑问句时，将 be 动词提前。若主语是第一人称，要改为第二人称。

I'm going to do the cleaning tomorrow. 我明天将要打扫卫生。

→ Are you going to do the cleaning tomorrow?
你明天会打扫卫生吗？

2. 含有 will 的一般将来时的变化

（1）变否定句时，直接在 will 后加 not。

There will be a movie this evening. 今天晚上将有一场电影。

→ There will not be a movie this evening. 今天晚上不会放映电影。

（2）变一般疑问句时，将 will 提前。若主语是第一人称，要改为第二人称。

I will do the cleaning tomorrow. 我明天将要打扫卫生。

→ Will you do the cleaning tomorrow? 你明天会打扫卫生吗？

Travel and Places

UNIT 2

语法大擂台

I. 完成下列句子，并与其相对应的图片连线。

1. Next summer holiday I _____ visit the Great Wall.

   A.

2. _____ you _____ _____ go to the library this afternoon?

   B.

3. My family _____ go to the farm next weekend.

   C.

4. _____ you clean the house tomorrow morning?

   D.

II. 翻译下列句子，并将其改为否定句和疑问句。

1. 我爸爸下个月要去参观纽约。（be going to）
   My father _____ _____ _____ _____ New York _____ _____.
   My father _____ _____ _____ _____ New York _____ _____.（否定句）
   _____ _____ _____ _____ _____ _____ New York _____ _____?

2. 这个小女孩明天要去学习游泳。（will）
   This little girl _____ _____ _____ _____ tomorrow.
   This little girl _____ _____ _____ _____ tomorrow.（否定句）
   _____ this little girl _____ _____ tomorrow?

日记导图秀

小朋友，你的家乡在哪里？你的家乡美吗？请你模仿上面的日记，写一篇关于家乡的日记吧！

_____ (Date)   _____ (Day)   _____ (Weather)

My Hometown

_____
_____
_____
_____
_____

UNIT 2 Travel and Places

参考范文

| January 23rd | Friday | Windy |

My Hometown

I was born in Shanghai. It is in the east of China. And it is one of the largest cities in China.

Shanghai is a popular city with many famous places. You can enjoy the beautiful night views around the Huangpu River. Last year, the Disney World was built in Shanghai, so you can visit it. I'm sure you will have a good time.

Shanghai is also a busy city. There are many cars on the road. If you want to travel around the city, you'd better take the subway.

词汇加油站

> 介绍一座城市还可能用到：

The people are friendly and kind. 人们善良而且友好。

It lies/is located in... 它坐落在……

The best way to travel around the city is... 游览这座城市的最好方式是……

...is famous for... ……以……闻名。

9. My School

| April 15th | Monday | Sunny |

My school is very beautiful.

There are three buildings — the teaching building, the library and the stadium. We study in the teaching building, and our classroom is in the third floor. There is also a big playground. We play games and do exercises on it. There is a basketball court, too. I often play basketball with my friends there after school.

I love my school.

Travel and Places

UNIT 2

好词妙妙屋

library 图书馆　　　stadium 体育馆　　　playground 运动场

do exercises 做操　　　　basketball court 篮球场
after school 放学后

参考译文

4月15日　　　　　　　星期一　　　　　　　晴

　　我的学校非常美丽。
　　我的学校有三座楼，分别是教学楼、图书馆和体育馆。我们在教学楼上课，我们班在三楼。学校还有一个运动场。我们常在那里做游戏、做操。我们学校还有一个篮球场，我和朋友放学后经常在那里打篮球。
　　我爱我的学校。

语法小贴士

　　多比学习汉语后发现，用汉语表达一般将来时，只需添加时间状语就可以，但是英语却不一样。表达不同的含义，所用的形式也不同。那么，我们今天就来了解一下一般将来时的用法吧！

1. 一般将来时表示将来发生的动作或状态。如：
   I will be ten years old next month. 下个月我就 10 岁了。
   She is going to have a piano class tomorrow. 她明天有一节钢琴课。

2. 表示预料要发生的事情。如：
   You will feel better after taking this medicine. 吃了这些药，你就会好一些。

3. 一些常用的表示将来的时间状语：next day/evening/month/week/year, in + 将来时间, tomorrow, in the future, from now on, this afternoon/weekend 等。
   I will go to the library this weekend. 我这周末要去图书馆。

语法大擂台

读句子，用一般将来时改写句子。

1. I often go to school by bike. (tomorrow)
   I _____ go to school by bike tomorrow.

2. There is a cinema in our city. (next year)
   There _____ a cinema in our city next year.

3. My father works in Beijing. (in 2020)
   My father _____ in Beijing in 2020.

4. We have six classes every day. (next term)
   We _____ six classes every day next term.

Travel and Places

UNIT 2

日记导图秀

小朋友，你喜欢你的学校吗？请你模仿上面的日记描述一下你的学校吧！

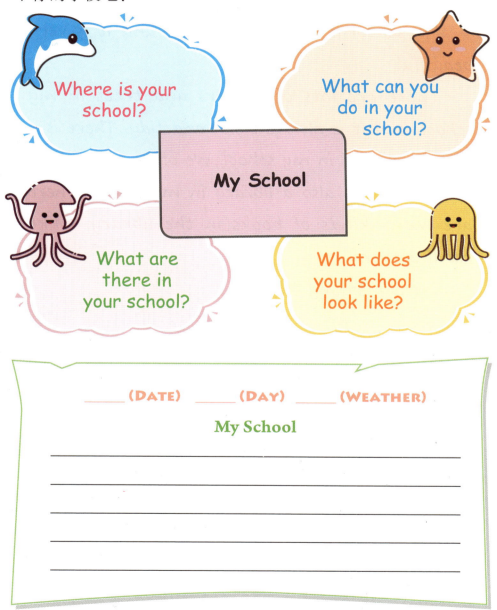

_____ (DATE) _____ (DAY) _____ (WEATHER)

My School

_____
_____
_____
_____
_____

参考范文

| July 25th | Friday | Sunny |

My School

My school is in Renmin Road, and it is very beautiful.

There are lots of flowers and trees in my school, and it is always clean and tidy. There is a big playground in my school. We often play sports on it. There is also a library in my school. There are many kinds of books in the library. I like reading there.

I really like my school.

词汇加油站

> 描写学校还可以用到:

The teachers in my school are strict.
我们学校的老师非常严厉。
The students are friendly. 学生很友好。
In school, I get along well with my classmates.
我在学校和同学相处得很好。
There are many trees around the school. 学校周围都是树。

10. Visiting Mount Tai

| August 15th | Thursday | Cloudy |

Today, I went to climb the Mount Tai with my father.

I wanted to watch the sunrise, so we didn't sleep last night. It took us three hours to get to the top. When we arrived, there were many people. Some people even brought the video to record the sunrise. When the sun began to come out, all the people were excited.

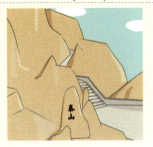

好词妙妙屋

sunrise 日出　　　　arrive 到达　　　　video 录像机
record 记录

It takes/took sb. some time to do sth. 做某事花了某人……时间
get to 到达　　　　　　　　come out 出来

参考译文

8月15日　　　　　　　星期四　　　　　　　多云

今天我和爸爸去爬泰山了。

我想去看日出，所以我们昨天晚上没有睡觉。我们花了三个小时才到达山顶。当我们到达山顶时，山上已经有很多人了。他们有的人甚至还带着录像机，要记录日出的瞬间。当太阳出来时，所有人都非常激动。

语法小贴士

肖明在学习英语时态时发现，用英语表达现在正在发生的动作还是比较简单的。只是有一点有些难——动词还是要发生变化，这让肖明有点头痛！看来想学好英语不是一件容易的事啊！我们今天就来学习一下现在进行时吧！

Travel and Places

UNIT 2

现在进行时的构成

现在进行时主要由 be(am, is, are)+doing 的形式构成。

1. I am reading a book. 我正在看书。

2. My mother is making a cake. 我妈妈正在做蛋糕。

3. The plane is flying in the sky. 飞机正在天上飞。

4. Those dogs are lying on the ground. 那些狗正躺在地上。

5. —What are you doing, children?
   孩子们，你们在做什么？
   —We are watching TV. 我们在看电视。

动词变 –ing 形式的规则

1. 大多数单词都是在词尾加 -ing。如：
   visit—visiting　look—looking

2. 以不发音的字母 e 结尾的动词，先去 e，再加 -ing。如：
   make—making　take—taking

3. 以"辅音+单个元音+辅音"结尾的单词，双写尾字母，再加 -ing。如：
   begin—beginning　stop—stopping

4. 以"-ie"结尾的单词，变 ie 为 y，再加 -ing。如：
   die—dying　lie—lying

语法大擂台

I. 写出下列动词的 -ing 形式，并与其对应的图片连线。

1. run _____

2. eat _____

3. close _____

4. cry _____

5. lie _____

6. rain _____

A.

B.

C.

D.

E.

F.

II. 根据图片提示完成句子。

1. Look! It _____ outside.

2. The girl _____.

3. Dobby and his father _____.

4. The girl _____.

Travel and Places

UNIT 2

日记导图秀

小朋友，你游览过哪些地方？请你模仿上面的日记描述一下吧！

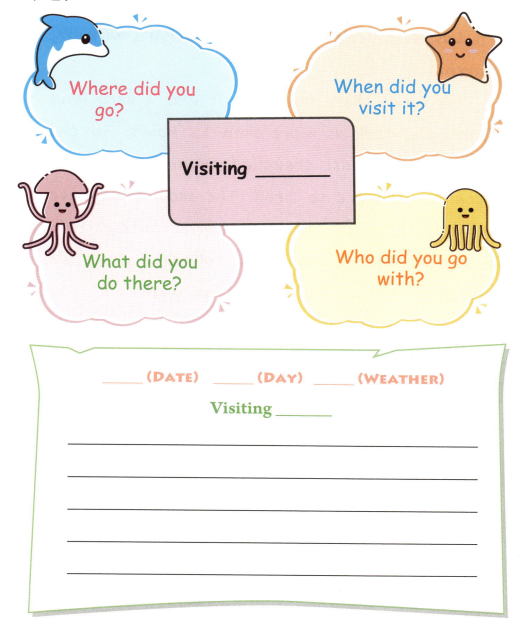

参考范文

| August 5th | Wednesday | Sunny |

Visiting Paris

Last summer holiday, I went to Paris with my parents.

We went there by plane. It was a very long journey. It took us more than 12 hours. For the first day, we just travelled around the hotel, because we were so tired. The second day, we went to the Eiffel Tower. It is beautiful especially when the light is on. In the following days, we visited the Louvre and bought many gifts.

We were very happy.

词汇加油站

> 在景区游玩时还可能用到:

I learned much knowledge about...
我学到了很多有关……的知识。

When we visit..., we must follow their customs.
当我们在……旅游时,我们必须遵循他们的风俗习惯。

We spent a week in... 我们在……游玩了一周。

Don't throw trash everywhere. 不要随地乱扔垃圾。

Unit 3
A Colorful Life

11. A Day in the Zoo

June 1st   **Sunday**   **Cloudy**

Today is Children's Day. My parents took my sister and me to the zoo.

There are many animals in the zoo. We first went to see the pandas. They were very cute. They were taking a bath. And then, we went to see the monkeys. They were very naughty. They were climbing the tree. We also watched the tigers, lions, bears and other animals.

We had a very good time there!

A Colorful Life

UNIT 3

好词妙妙屋

zoo 动物园　　　　　cute 可爱的　　　　naughty 淘气的
tiger 老虎　　　　　　lion 狮子　　　　　　bear 熊
take a bath 洗澡　　　　climb the tree 爬树

参考译文

6月1日　　　　　　星期日　　　　　　多云

今天是六一儿童节。我爸爸妈妈带着我和妹妹去了动物园。

动物园里有很多动物。我们首先去看了熊猫。它们非常可爱。当时它们正在洗澡。然后我们去看了猴子。它们非常淘气。当时它们正在爬树。我们还去看了老虎、狮子、熊和其他动物。

我们在那里玩得很开心。

语法小贴士

小朋友们，你们记住动词 -ing 形式的变化规则了吗？在表达现在进行时的句子中，动词 -ing 不可或缺，非常重要。所以小朋友们一定要记住哦！掌握了动词 -ing 形式的变化规则，我们开始学习现在进行时的用法。

现在进行时的用法

1. 现在进行时表示正在进行的动作，常与 now 连用，有时前边有 look, listen 等提示词。

   She is playing the piano now. 她正在弹钢琴。

   Listen! Who is singing? 听！是谁在唱歌？

2. 表示当前或近一个阶段一直或反复进行的动作或难以终止的动作。

   We are learning Lesson 12 this week. 我们本周正在学习第12课。

3. 表示经常反复的动作，常与 always 连用，表达赞扬或厌恶等情绪，使句子带有强烈的感情色彩。

   He is always helping others. 他总是在帮助别人。

4. 表示明确安排好了的、不久将要发生的事情，表示将来的动作（时常有一个表示未来时间的状语）。

   We are leaving on Friday. 我们星期五走。

   注意：仅有少量动词有这种用法，如：start, go, come, arrive 等。

语法大擂台

读一读下面的句子，根据图片补全句子。

1. The girl is _____.

2. The boy is _____.

3. The monkey is _____.

A Colorful Life

3 UNIT

4. The elephant is _____.

5. Our family are _____.

日记导图秀

小朋友，你去过公园吗？请你模仿上面的日记描述一下吧！

_____(Date) _____(Day) _____(Weather)

A Day in the Park

参考范文 11

May 7th　　　**Sunday**　　　**Sunny**

A Day in the Park

This afternoon, my parents and I went to the park.

The park is not very big, but it is beautiful. There are many kinds of flowers and trees. This afternoon, there were many people in it. Several young men were running. Two old men were playing chess. There was a group of old people dancing by the lake. Some children were playing with toys.

All the people had a good time.

A Colorful Life

UNIT 3

词汇加油站

> 描述一天的活动还可能用到：

I did some cleaning today.
今天我做了一些清洁的工作。

I went shopping with my mother.
我和妈妈去购物了。

I helped my mother make the dinner.
我帮助妈妈做了晚饭。

I went to the park to fly a kite with my friend.
我去公园和我的朋友一起放风筝。

I read a book in the library.
我在图书馆看了一本书。

12. My Birthday Party

April 27th　　　**Saturday**　　　**Sunny**

 Today is my birthday. I will hold a birthday party in my house. I will invite my friends, too.

 In the morning, I will sweep the floor, clean the table, and tidy up my toys. In the afternoon, I will go shopping with my father. We will buy some candies. My mother will be at home. She will make a birthday cake and some cookies for us.

 I hope I will have a happy birthday party.

A Colorful Life

UNIT 3

好词妙妙屋

hold 举办　　　　invite 邀请　　　　sweep 打扫
candy 糖果　　　　cookie 小饼干

tidy up 整理，收拾　　　　go shopping 去购物

参考译文

4月27日　　　　　　星期六　　　　　　晴

　　今天是我的生日。我要在家举办一个生日聚会，我还会邀请我的朋友们。

　　上午，我会扫地、擦桌子、整理玩具。下午，我会和爸爸去购物，我们要买一些糖果。妈妈会在家为我们做生日蛋糕和小饼干。

　　我希望能举办一个快乐的生日聚会。

语法小贴士

　　小朋友，我们已经学习并掌握了有关英语词法的知识，也了解了时态的基本知识，今天我们继续学习句法。在汉语中，句子主要分为陈述句、疑问句、祈使句和感叹句四大类，英语句子也分为这四类。今天我们重点学习一下陈述句的用法。

陈述句是指说明事实或陈述说话人观点的句子。

基本结构为：**主语 + 谓语动词 + 其他成分**

I study English. 我学习英语。（主语 + 谓语 + 宾语）

My car broke down. 我的车出故障了。（主语 + 谓语）

My mother asked me to clean the house. 我妈妈让我打扫房间。（主语 + 谓语 + 宾语 + 宾语补足语）

My mother told me a story. 我妈妈给我讲了一个故事。（主语 + 谓语 + 间接宾语 + 直接宾语）

I am a student. 我是一名学生。（主语 + 系动词 + 表语）

以上几个句子是我们常见的陈述句结构，我们在写作文时都可以用到。

语法大擂台

根据汉语提示，完成英语句子。

1. 我每天早上 7 点去上学。

   I _____ _____ _____ at 7 o'clock in the morning.

2. 我家有四口人。

   _____ _____ four people in my family.

3. 我今天下午要去公园。

   _____ _____ _____ _____ the park this afternoon.

4. 我妈妈给我买了一条新裙子。

   My mother _____ me _____ _____ _____.

5. 妈妈让我收拾玩具。

   My mother _____ me _____ _____ _____ my toys.

A Colorful Life

UNIT 3

日记导图秀

小朋友，你举办过或参加过生日会吗？请你模仿上面的日记描述一下吧！

_____ (Date) _____ (Day) _____ (Weather)

A Birthday Party

_____
_____
_____
_____

参考范文

April 27th   **Saturday**   **Sunny**

A Birthday Party

Today is Dobby's birthday. He invited me to take part in his birthday party. I was very happy.

This afternoon, I went to buy an easy camera. I hoped he would record the happy time by taking photos. I went to his house at a quarter to 6. And the party began at 6. There were many friends. We sang a "Happy birthday" song for him. After that we ate birthday cake. It was very delicious. We had a very happy time there.

词汇加油站

> 描写生日还可能用到：

make a wish 许愿
light/blow the candles 点/吹蜡烛
divide the cake 切蛋糕
make a birthday card 做生日贺卡
Wish all your dreams come true!
祝你梦想成真！

13. On Duty

April 11th   Thursday   Sunny

I was on duty today. After school, when other students went home, I began to do the cleaning.

I first cleaned the blackboard. Then I swept and mopped the floor. After that I put the desks and chairs in order. Everything looks very tidy.

I turned off the lights, locked the door and went back home.

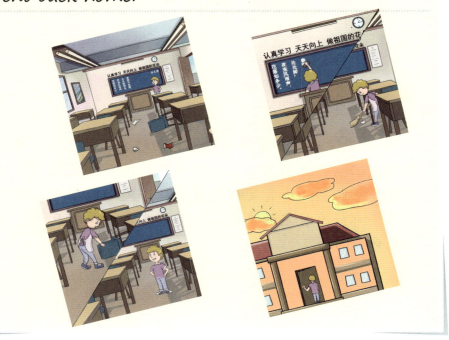

我的英语日记书 提高篇

好词妙妙屋

blackboard 黑板　　sweep 清扫　　mop 用拖把拖
tidy 整洁的　　lock 锁

on duty 值日　　　　　　put... in order 将……摆放整齐
turn off 关闭

参考译文

4月11日　　　　　星期四　　　　　　　晴

　　今天我值日。同学们放学回家后，我开始打扫教室。
　　我先擦黑板，然后扫地、拖地。之后我将桌椅摆放整齐。一切都非常整洁了。
　　我关上灯、锁好门，然后回家了。

语法小贴士

　　小朋友，我们知道陈述句家族的职责是叙述一个事实。其特点是句末用句号，朗读时通常用降调。陈述句家族中有两个"兄弟"：肯定句是哥哥，否定句是弟弟。哥哥对人对事都持有肯定的态度，而弟弟常和哥哥唱反调，总是否定哥哥的话。

A Colorful Life

UNIT 3

陈述句的否定形式

1. 在含有 be 动词的陈述句中，变否定句时，直接在 be 动词后加 not。如：

    I am a student. 我是一名学生。

    → I'm not a student. 我不是一名学生。

2. 在含有情态动词的陈述句中，变否定句时，直接在情态动词后加 not。如：

    I can swim. 我会游泳。

    → I can't swim. 我不会游泳。

3. 在含有实义动词的陈述句中，变否定句时，要借助于助动词 do 的适当形式，在 do 的后面加 not，实义动词变为原形。如：

    My father works in a factory. 我爸爸在一家工厂上班。

    → My father doesn't work in a factory. 我爸爸不在工厂上班。

陈述句的疑问句形式

1. 在含有 be 动词的陈述句中，直接将 be 动词提前至句首，如主语是第一人称，变疑问句时改为第二人称。如：

    I am a student. 我是一名学生。

    → Are you a student? 你是一名学生吗？

2. 在含有情态动词的陈述句中，直接将情态动词提前至句首，如主语是第一人称，变疑问句时改为第二人称。如：

    I can swim. 我会游泳。

    → Can you swim? 你会游泳吗？

3. 在含有实义动词的陈述句中，借助于助动词 do 的适当形式，将其放在句首，实义动词变为原形，如主语是第一人称，变疑问句时改为第二人称。如：

    My father works in a factory. 我爸爸在一家工厂上班。

    → Does your father work in a factory? 你爸爸在工厂上班吗？

语法大擂台

按要求改写句子。

1. I live in Beijing.（改为一般疑问句）
   _____ _____ live in Beijing?
2. My mother made a cake for me.（改为否定句）
   My mother _____ _____ a cake for me.
3. Lucy can play the piano very well.（改为否定句）
   Lucy _____ _____ the piano very well.
4. Tom can run very fast.（改为一般疑问句）
   _____ _____ _____ very fast?
5. I will go to school tomorrow.（改为一般疑问句）
   _____ _____ _____ to school tomorrow?

日记导图秀

小朋友，你在家里做过家务吗？请你模仿上面的日记描述一下吧！

Why do you clean the house?

What did you do?

Cleaning the House

Who did the cleaning with you?

…

___(DATE) ___(DAY) ___(WEATHER)

Cleaning the House

参考范文  13

| January 25th | Tuesday | Sunny |

Cleaning the House

Spring Festival is coming. My family decided to have a thorough cleaning.

My mother tidied up the kitchen. My father cleaned the bathroom. I cleaned the living room and my bedroom. I first cleaned the window and table. Then I swept and mopped the floor. After half an hour, the house became neat and tidy.

I felt tired after cleaning the rooms, but I was very happy.

词汇加油站

> **描写劳动还可能会用到：**

　　take out the trash 倒垃圾

　　make the bed 铺床

　　cook the meal 做饭

　　wash the dishes/clothes 洗碗/衣服

　　water the flowers 浇花

> **与劳动相关的谚语：**

　　No pains, no gains. 没有付出就没有收获。
　　A harvest comes from a hard work.
　　一分耕耘，一分收获。
　　How much sweat, how much food.
　　流多少汗，吃多少饭。

A Colorful Life

UNIT 3

 # 14. Sports Meeting

September 19th   Thursday   Sunny

It was a sunny day today. We watched a sports meeting in the school playground.

Four boys from our class took part in the boys' relay. They got the first place. Chen Jie runs fastest in our class. She joined in the girls' 100-meter race and won it. Fang Qun took part in the long jump, and he got the second place.

It was a very successful sports meeting. All of us were very happy.

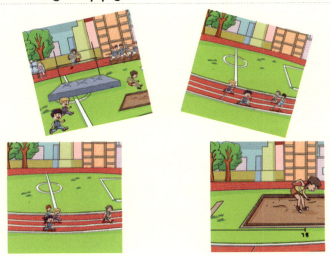

好词妙妙屋

relay 接力赛　　　　fast 快地　　　win 获胜
successful 成功的

take part in 参加　　　　　　　join in 参加
100-meter race 100 米赛跑　　　long jump 跳远

参考译文

9月19日　　　　　　星期四　　　　　　晴

今天天气晴朗。我们在学校的运动场上观看了一场运动会。

我们班有4名男生参加了男子接力比赛，并获得了第一名。陈洁在我们班跑得最快，她参加了女子百米赛跑，并赢得了比赛。方群参加了男子跳远比赛，他获得了第二名。

这是一次非常成功的运动会，我们都很高兴。

语法小贴士

多比来到中国后，发现了一个很奇怪的现象：人们见面打招呼时通常说"你吃了吗？"这让他感到很奇怪，怎么用疑问句打招呼呢？英语中的疑问句家族主要有三兄弟——一般疑问句、特殊疑问句和选择疑问句。

UNIT 3 A Colorful Life

1. 一般疑问句通常以 be 动词、情态动词或助动词开头，其回答要用 Yes 或 No。如：

   —Are you a student? 你是一名学生吗？
   —Yes, I am. 是的，我是。
   —No, I'm not. 不，我不是。
   —Can you swim? 你会游泳吗？
   —Yes, I can. 是的，我会。
   —No, I can't. 不，我不会。
   —Will you go to school tomorrow? 你明天去上学吗？
   —Yes, I will. 是的，我去上学。
   —No, I won't. 不，我不去上学。
   —Do you like playing the guitar? 你喜欢弹吉他吗？
   —Yes, I do. 是的，我喜欢。
   —No, I don't. 不，我不喜欢。

2. 特殊疑问句是以特殊疑问词开头的疑问句，特殊疑问词主要包括 what, why, which, when, where, who, whose, how 等。如：

   What's your name? 你叫什么名字？
   Where do you come from? 你从哪里来？
   Why are you late for school? 你为什么上学迟到了？
   How do you feel today? 你今天感觉怎么样？
   When do you go to school？你什么时候去上学？
   Who's the boy under the tree? 树下的男孩是谁？

3. 选择疑问句一般提供两个或两个以上的选项，供对方选择，供选择的对象用 or 连接。如：

   Which bag is yours, the red one or the blue one?
   哪个书包是你的，红色的还是蓝色的？
   Would you like a cup of tea or coffee? 你想喝茶还是咖啡？

语法大擂台

帮小蝌蚪找妈妈。

A. Is she singing in the classroom?

B. Do you like apples or bananas?

C. When will you start working?

D. Which boy is your brother, the tall one or the short one?

E. Could you help me?

F. Who is the woman with a pair of glasses?

一般疑问句　　特殊疑问句　　选择疑问句

A Colorful Life

UNIT 3

日记导图秀

小朋友，你们学校开运动会时，你参加运动项目了吗？取得成绩了吗？请你模仿上面的日记描述一下吧！

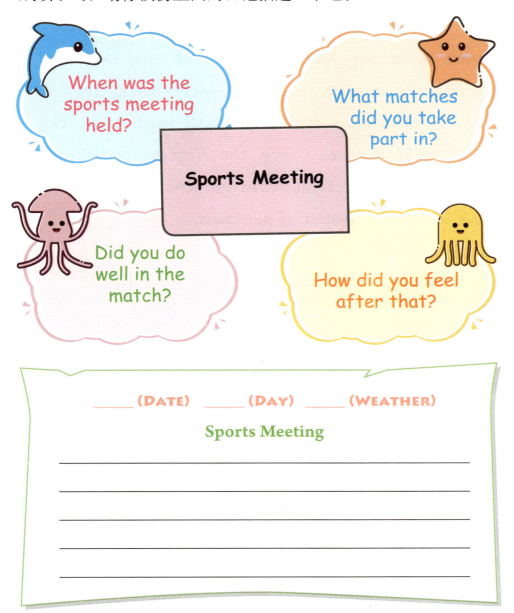

When was the sports meeting held?

What matches did you take part in?

Sports Meeting

Did you do well in the match?

How did you feel after that?

_____ (DATE) _____ (DAY) _____ (WEATHER)

Sports Meeting

_____
_____
_____
_____
_____

参考范文

October 21st   Wednesday   Sunny

Sports Meeting

Today, my school held a sports meeting. I took part in several matches, so I was very excited. I took part in 100- and 400-meter race. Besides, I also joined in the basketball match. In the 100-meter race, I won the first place. What's more, our basketball team got the second place. We were very proud of our class.

词汇加油站

> 运动会的项目还有：

high jump 跳高   shot put 掷铅球

long jump 跳远   marathon 马拉松

shooting 射击   diving 跳水

> 在运动会上可能会发生：

Our class broke the school's record.
我们班打破了学校纪录。

I joined in the cheer team. 我加入了啦啦队。

I helped the players carry their belongings.
我帮运动员拿私人物品。

15. My First Day at School

June 28th   Friday   Sunny

    Today I watched a graduation ceremony at school. It reminded me of my first day at school.

    When I went to school in the first day, my parents drove me to school. I walked to the classroom with them. After half an hour, they went away. I felt very sad and lonely. But soon I forgot the unhappiness, because I made new friends.

我的英语日记书 提高篇

好词妙妙屋

watch 观看　　　　remind 使记起　　　　drive 开车
lonely 孤独的　　　unhappiness 不愉快

graduation ceremony 毕业典礼
It reminded sb. of sth. 使某人想起某事
go away 离开　　　　　　make friends 交朋友

参考译文

6月28日　　　　　星期五　　　　　　晴

　　今天我在学校观看了一场毕业典礼。这使我想起了我第一天上学的情景。

　　我第一天上学是我爸爸妈妈开车送我去的学校。我和他们一起走进了教室。半小时后,他们离开了。我感到既伤心又孤独。不过我很快就忘记了这些不愉快,因为我交到了新朋友。

语法小贴士

　　我们和别人打招呼时经常说"你吃了吗?"在汉语中这就是一般疑问句。那么,你们知道如何用英语表达"你吃了吗?"今天,我们就带大家走进一般疑问句的世界,一起感受一下一般疑问句的魅力。

A Colorful Life

UNIT 3

定义及构成

用 Yes 或 No 作答的疑问句叫一般疑问句。其基本结构为：be 动词 / 助动词 / 情态动词 + 主语 + 谓语 / 表语 +（其他）。

Is she singing in the classroom? 她是在教室里唱歌吗？

Can you swim? 你会游泳吗？

Do you go to school by bike? 你骑自行车上学吗？

回答

一般疑问句有两种回答方式，分别是肯定回答和否定回答。

肯定回答一般用"Yes, 主语 +be 动词 / 助动词 / 情态动词"表示；否定回答一般用"No, 主语 +be 动词 / 助动词 / 情态动词 +not"表示。

—Can you swim? 你会游泳吗？

—Yes, I can./No, I can't. 是的，我会。/ 不，我不会。

语法大擂台

给下列句子作肯定或否定回答。

1. Are you a student?（作肯定回答）

   _____

2. Are you playing football?（作否定回答）

   _____

3. Do you live in Beijing?（作肯定回答）

   _____

4. Will you go to school tomorrow?（作否定回答）

   _____

日记导图秀

小朋友，你还记得你第一天上学或开学第一天的场景吗？请模仿上面的日记描述一下吧！

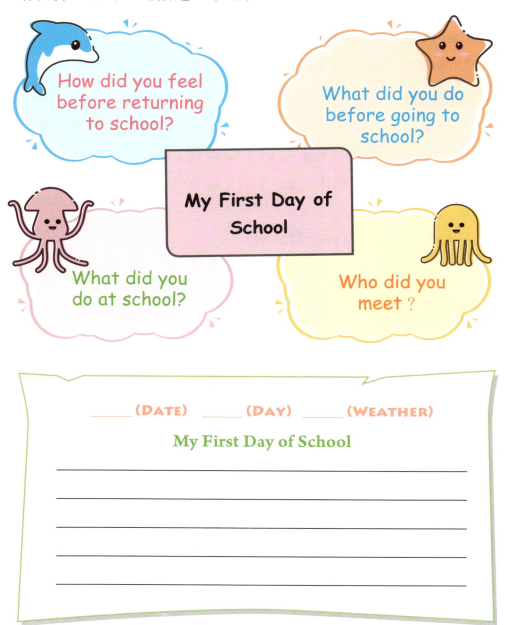

_____ (DATE) _____ (DAY) _____ (WEATHER)

My First Day of School

UNIT 3 A Colorful Life

 15

| September 1st | Monday | Sunny |

My First Day of School

It was the first day of school. I really wanted to go back to school at once. I wanted to meet my teachers and friends.

I got up very early in the morning and then rode to school. Today our teacher introduced a new student to us. He was Dobby Black, from Australia. He became my deskmate. And we became good friends soon.

词汇加油站

▶ 开学或上学第一天可能会发生：

I didn't know anyone at school, so I felt very lonely.
我在学校不认识任何人，所以我感到很孤独。

On my first day at school, I met one of my friends from kindergarten.
上学第一天，我遇到了我在幼儿园时的一个朋友。

We had a new English teacher this term.
我们这学期有一位新的英语老师。

Unit 4
Beautiful Nature

16. The River in My Hometown

January 16th   Wednesday   Sunny

There is a river in my hometown. In the past, people could see fishes, shrimps and crabs in it. We often went there to swim in summer.

But now it's smelly and dirty, and nobody goes there to swim and play. What a pity! On weekends, my friends always go there to pick up rubbish. I hope people will do something to protect the environment.

Beautiful Nature

UNIT 4

好词妙妙屋

shrimp 虾　　　　crab 螃蟹　　　　smelly 难闻的
rubbish 垃圾

What a pity! 太遗憾了!　　　pick up 捡，拾
protect the environment 保护环境

参考译文

1月16日　　　　　星期三　　　　　晴

　　我的家乡有一条小河。在过去，人们可以看见河里的鱼、虾和螃蟹。在夏天，我们经常去河里游泳。

　　但是现在，河水又脏又臭，所以没有人去那里游泳和玩耍了。真是太遗憾了！在周末，我的朋友们经常去河边捡垃圾。我希望人们能够做些事来保护环境。

语法小贴士

　　我们在英语对话中经常用到"What's your name?""When do you go to school?""Why are you late?"这样的句子。这种含有what、when、why等特殊疑问词的句子叫作特殊疑问句。今天我们给大家介绍一下几个常用的特殊疑问词的含义及用法。

what 常用于询问东西、事情，意为"什么"。

—What are you doing? 你在做什么？

—I am reading a book. 我在看书。

—What is this? 这是什么？

—It's a book. 这是一本书。

who 和 whom 常用于询问人，who 既可以作主语也可以作宾语，whom 只能作宾语。

—Who is the boy under the tree? 树底下的小男孩是谁？

—He's my brother. 他是我的弟弟。

—Who/Whom do you like best? 你最喜欢谁？

—I like my mother best. 我最喜欢妈妈。

whose 常用于询问所属关系，意为"谁的"。

—Whose bag is it? 这个书包是谁的？

—It's Tom's. 这是汤姆的。

which 常用于选择，意为"哪一个"。

—Which one do you like, the red one or the blue one? 你喜欢哪一个，红色的还是蓝色的？

—I like the red one. 我喜欢红色的。

when 用于询问时间，意为"什么时候"。

—When do you usually go to school? 你通常什么时候去上学？

—I usually go to school at 7：30. 我通常7点半去上学。

where 用于询问地点，意为"在哪里"。

—Where is your hometown? 你的家乡在哪里？

—My hometown is in Sydney 我的家乡在悉尼。

Beautiful Nature

UNIT 4

how 用于询问方式、手段、程度等，意为"如何"。

—How do you feel? 你感觉如何？

—I feel much better. 我感觉好多了。

—How do you usually go to school? 你通常怎样去上学？

—I usually go to school by bus. 我通常乘公交车去上学。

why 用于询问原因，意为"为什么"。

—Why did you get up late? 你为什么起晚了？

—Because I stayed up. 因为我熬夜了。

语法大擂台

读对话，根据答语用正确的疑问词填空。

Tony: _____ are we going this winter holiday?

Dad: We will go to Harbin.

Tony: _____ are we going to Harbin?

Dad: On 21st January.

Tony: _____ do we go there?

Dad: We will go there by plane.

Tony: _____ are we going to do there?

Dad: We will watch the ice sculptures (冰雕).

Tony: _____ season do you like in Harbin?

Dad: I like winter.

Tony: _____?

Dad: Because we can skate and make snowmen.

日记导图秀

小朋友，你去过农村吗？你认为农村漂亮吗？请你模仿上面的日记自己描述一下吧！

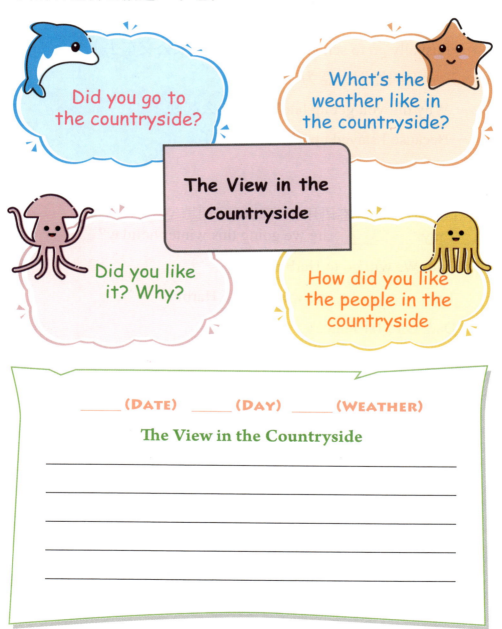

_____(DATE) _____(DAY) _____(WEATHER)

The View in the Countryside

Unit 4 Beautiful Nature

参考范文

June 1st　　　　Saturday　　　　Sunny

The View in the Countryside

When I was young, I lived in the countryside with my grandparents. I loved there very much.

Early in the morning, the air was very fresh, and I could hear the birds singing in the tree. At dusk, the setting sun was very big and it looked like a burning ball. In the evening, there were many stars shining in the sky. The scenery in the countryside was so beautiful!

词汇加油站

> 描写乡村还可能用到：

wonderful 美妙的，极好的
amazing 令人惊奇的　　　peaceful 宁静的
The country is very green in spring.
乡村的春天一片青葱碧绿。
Flocks of sheep and cows are eating grass leisurely in the field. 成群的牛羊在田野里悠闲地吃着草。

17. My Favorite Animal

July 19th   Friday   Sunny

Of all animals, I like panda best. I think panda is the most lovely animal in the world. It is considered as the treasure of China. It has a round body shape and eyes with black rim. Bamboos are its favorite food. Most pandas live in Sichuan, China, and there is a Panda Park in Chengdu.

Panda is often treated as ambassador to visit other countries. People around the world love this cute animal.

Beautiful Nature

UNIT 4

好词妙妙屋

lovely 可爱的　　　treasure 珍宝　　　bamboo 竹子
treat 对待　　　　 ambassador 大使　　cute 可爱的

be considered as... 被看作……
eyes with black rim 带黑眼圈的眼睛
Panda Park 熊猫乐园　　　　　　　be treated as... 被当作……

参考译文

7月19日　　　　　星期五　　　　　　晴

在所有动物中，我最喜欢大熊猫。我认为熊猫是世界上最可爱的动物。它被看作是中国的国宝。它拥有滚圆的体型和带黑眼圈的眼睛。竹子是它最喜欢的食物。大部分熊猫生活在中国四川，成都还有一个熊猫乐园。

熊猫常被当作访问其他国家的外交大使。全世界的人们都喜欢这个可爱的动物。

语法小贴士

小朋友们，我们已经学习了疑问句中的一般疑问句和特殊疑问句。当我们提出两种或两种以上的情况，并要求对方选择一种情况时，我们就要用到选择疑问句。

> 选择疑问句中连接两种或两种以上的情况用 or，回答时不能用 yes 或 no，要么从前面提到的情况中选择一个，要么都不选择，另外提出一个新情况。选择疑问句可以分为一般选择疑问句和特殊选择疑问句两种。

一般选择疑问句

结构：一般疑问句 + or + 被选择的情况？

—Are you a teacher or a student? 你是老师还是学生？

—I'm a student. 我是个学生。

—Did you work out the math problem in this way or (in) that way?
你用这种方法还是用那种方法把这道数学题算出来的？

—I did it in that way. 我用那种方法算出来的。

特殊选择疑问句

结构：特殊疑问句，A or B？

—Which city is bigger, Beijing or New York?
哪个城市更大些，北京还是纽约？

—Beijing. 北京。

—When will he leave for London, today or tomorrow?
他何时动身去伦敦，今天还是明天？

—Tomorrow. 明天。

Beautiful Nature

UNIT 4

语法大擂台

根据图片提示，完成句子。

1. —Is your mother a teacher or a nurse?
   —A _____.

2. —Did you play the piano or the violin yesterday?
   —Neither. I played the _____.

3. —Which city will you go to on vacation, Beijing or London?
   —Beijing. Because I want to visit _____.

4. —Which subject do you like, English or math?
   —_____.

5. —Do you go to school by bus or by bike?
   —_____.

我的英语日记书 提高篇

日记导图秀

小朋友，你最喜欢哪种动物？请你模仿上面的日记描写一下你最喜欢的动物吧！

_____(DATE) _____(DAY) _____(WEATHER)

My Favorite Animal

Beautiful Nature

Unit 4

参考范文 🎧 17

January 31st   Saturday   Sunny

My Favorite Animal

Do you like animals? What's your favorite animal? My favorite animal is the monkey. It has a long tail. The tail is very useful for the monkey. It can hang upside down on a tree with its tail. The monkey is very lovely and clever. It can imitate people's actions. It likes eating bananas. It can peel off the skin of the bananas. I love it so much!

词汇加油站

> 常见的动物还有：

tiger 老虎	lion 狮子	cat 猫
dog 狗	parrot 鹦鹉	fish 鱼
kangaroo 袋鼠	koala 考拉	horse 马

> 描写动物还可能用到：

They live in the forest. 它们生活在森林中。
They live on vegetables. 它们以蔬菜为食。
It is the largest/smallest animal. 它是最大/最小的动物。

18. Winter Is Coming!

December 25th   **Thursday**   **Snowy**

This morning, when I got up and opened the curtain, I found the outside was covered by white. The trees were white, the road was white, the houses were white, and everything was white.

A group of children were playing happily. Some were throwing snowballs to each other. Some were making a snowman.

Winter is coming!

Beautiful Nature

UNIT 4

好词妙妙屋

curtain 窗帘　　　　cover 覆盖　　　　everything 一切
throw 扔　　　　　 snowball 雪球

get up 起床　　　　　　　　be covered by... 被……覆盖
each other 互相　　　　　　make a snowman 堆雪人

参考译文

12月25日　　　　星期四　　　　　　雪

　　我今天早上起床打开窗帘后，发现外面变成了白色的世界。树是白色的，马路是白色的，房屋也是白色的，一切都是白色的。

　　一些小孩在外面高兴地玩耍。有些在打雪仗，有些在堆雪人。

　　冬天来了！

语法小贴士

　　在我们上课前，老师到来时，值日生经常说的"起立"（stand up）；或者我们在赶时间时经常听见的"快点"（hurry up）。这些都是表示命令的话语，这就是我们今天要学习的祈使句。

祈使句的含义及构成

　　祈使句通常用来表示请求、命令、建议、禁止等含义。祈使句通常没有主语，以动词原形开头。

　　Please open the door. 请打开窗户。（表请求）

Stand up! 起立！（表命令）

Let's go fishing! 我们去钓鱼吧！（表建议）

Keep off the grass! 勿踏草坪！（表禁止）

祈使句的否定形式

祈使句有两种否定形式，一种是 Don't + 动词原形，另一种是 No + 动词 ing 形式或 No + 名词复数形式。

Don't swim here. 不要在这里游泳。

No parking here! 这里禁止停车！

No photos! 禁止拍照！

语法大擂台

读句子，选择与句子内容相符的图片，并连线。

1. Let's have a picnic tomorrow.　　A.

2. No photos!　　B.

3. Go and wash your hands.　　C.

4. Don't touch, please.　　D.

5. No smoking!　　E.

Beautiful Nature

Unit 4

日记导图秀

小朋友，你有没有特别喜欢或讨厌的天气？能告诉大家为什么吗？请你模仿上面的日记自己写一写吧！

What weather do you like the most/least?

What does it look like in such weather?

Why do you like/dislike it?

How do you feel when it is…?

_____ (DATE) _____ (DAY) _____ (WEATHER)

_____
_____
_____
_____
_____

参考范文

July 21st   Saturday   Rainy

I Hate Rainy Days!

This morning, when I got up and opened the curtain, I found it was raining outside. What a pity!

My friends and I planned to have a picnic today, but it had to be cancelled because of the bad weather. I have to stay at home to do my homework. So boring! I hate rainy days!

词汇加油站

▶ 描写下雨天还可能用到：

dark cloud 乌云　　lightning 闪电
thunder 雷　　rainbow 彩虹

The road was filled with puddles from the rain.
雨后路面上到处是水坑。

It rained cats and dogs last night.
昨天晚上雨下得很大。

After the rainstorm, there is a rainbow in the sky.
暴雨过后，天空中出现了一道彩虹。

Beautiful Nature

19. A Clever Crow

| August 3rd | Saturday | Sunny |

Today I read a story about a clever crow.

The crow was very thirsty after a long journey. He looked for water here and there. At last he found a bottle, but there was only a little water. He got a good idea. He put some small stones into the bottle, and the water rose. The crow drank the water and he was very happy.

我的英语日记书 提高篇

好词妙妙屋

crow 乌鸦　　　thirsty 口渴的　　journey 旅途
stone 石头　　　rise 上升

look for 寻找　　　　　　here and there 到处
at last 最后　　　　　　　put sth. into sth. 把……放入……

参考译文

8月3日　　　　　　星期六　　　　　　　晴

　　我今天读了一篇关于一只聪明的乌鸦的故事。
　　这只乌鸦长途旅行后非常口渴，于是他到处找水喝。最后他看见了一个瓶子，但是瓶子里只有一点水。这只乌鸦想到了一个好主意。他把小石子放进瓶子里，于是里面的水上升了。乌鸦喝到水了，他非常高兴。

语法小贴士

　　我们去旅游时，当发现非常漂亮的景色时，常会发出"哇！好美啊！"这样的感叹。当我们要表达强烈的感情时，我们就会用到感叹句。感叹句是表达感慨、惊叹，体现人的喜、怒、哀、乐等强烈感情的句子。感叹句主要有两种表达形式：

Beautiful Nature

UNIT 4

1. **由 what 引导**

   结构：What + a(n) + *adj.* + *n.*(单数) + (主语 + 谓语)!

   What + *adj.* + *n.*(复数/不可数) + (主语 + 谓语)!

   What a pretty girl (she is)! 多漂亮的一个女孩啊！

   What beautiful flowers! 这些花真漂亮啊！

   What heavy snow! 好大的雪啊！

2. **由 how 引导**

   结构：How + *adj./adv.* + (主语 + 谓语)!

   How pretty the bear is! 好漂亮的一只小熊啊！

   How slowly it walks! 它走得好慢啊！

语法大擂台

读一读下面的句子，用 what 或 how 填空。

1. _____ a nice dress!

2. _____ heavy the box is!

3. _____ quickly they fly!

4. _____ an important meeting it is!

5. _____ lovely frogs they are!

我的英语日记书 提高篇

日记导图秀

小朋友，你听说过狐狸和乌鸦的故事吗？请你模仿上面的日记描述一下吧！

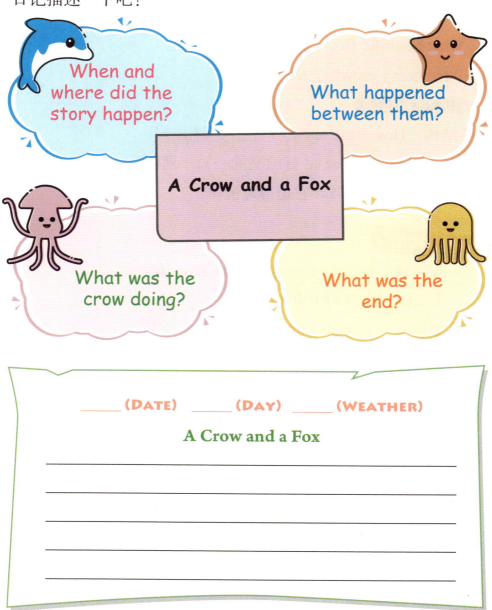

_____(Date) _____(Day) _____(Weather)

A Crow and a Fox

UNIT 4 Beautiful Nature

| August 26th | Thursday | Rainy |

A Crow and a Fox

Today, my mother told me a story about a crow and a fox.

A fox was very hungry, and he was looking for food. Suddenly he saw a crow standing in the tree. There was a piece of meat in her mouth. The fox wanted to get the meat. He said to the crow, "Miss Crow, you sing very well. So could you sing a song for me?" Hearing this, the crow was very happy. The meat dropped as soon as she opened the mouth. The fox picked up the meat and ran away.

词汇加油站

> 有关动物的故事还有：

The Turtle and the Hare 龟兔赛跑

The Fox and the Tiger 狐假虎威

The Little Horse Crosses the River 小马过河

Three Pigs 三只小猪

20. How to Protect the Environment

July 23rd　　　　　Tuesday　　　　　Sunny

Today, I saw a picture in the gallery. It was an eagle standing on the desert, thirsty.

Now the environment problems are becoming more and more serious. We must try our best to protect it. We should not cut down trees, but plant more trees. In order to keep the water clean, we shouldn't throw the rubbish into the river. If everyone can make contribution to the environment, our home will become more and more beautiful!

Beautiful Nature

UNIT 4

好词妙妙屋

protect 保护　　gallery 美术馆　　eagle 老鹰
desert 沙漠　　serious 严重的

try one's best to do 尽某人最大努力做　　cut down 砍伐
make contribution 做贡献

参考译文

7月23日　　　　星期二　　　　　晴

　　今天我在美术馆看到了一幅画。画里是一只老鹰站在沙漠中，它非常口渴。

　　现在，环境问题越来越严重。我们必须尽力保护它。我们不应该砍树，而是要多植树。为了保持河水干净，我们不应该向河里倾倒垃圾。如果每个人都能为环境贡献一份力，我们的家园就会变得越来越美丽！

语法小贴士

　　肖明在学习英语时又遇到了新问题，在表达"我有一支钢笔。"时他会说"I have a pen."但是当他用"The house has many people."时，老师却说他错了。小朋友们，你们知道肖明错在哪里了吗？我们用英语表达某地有或存在某物时，应该用 There be 句型。

1. There be 句型的结构

    There be + 某物 / 某人 + 某地

    There is a desk in my bedroom. 我的卧室里有一张桌子。

    There are some students in the classroom. 教室里有一些学生。

2. There be 句型的疑问句和否定句形式

    (1) There be 句型变一般疑问句时，将 be 动词提前即可。句中含有第一人称时，改为第二人称；若有 some，改成 any。

    There is a desk in my bedroom. 我的卧室里有一张桌子。

    →Is there a desk in your bedroom? 你的卧室里有一张桌子吗?

    (2) There be 句型变否定句时，在 be 动词后加 not。句中若有 some，改成 any。

    There is not a desk in my bedroom. 我的卧室里没有桌子。

    There are some students in the classroom. 教室里有一些学生。

    →There are not any students in the classroom. 教室里没有学生。

语法大擂台

按要求改写句子。

1. There is a book in my bag.（改为一般疑问句，并作肯定回答）

    _____ _____ a book in _____ bag?

    _____, _____ _____.

2. There are some apples in the basket.（改为一般疑问句，并作否定回答）

    _____ _____ _____ apples in the basket?

    _____, _____ _____.

3. There is a river in my hometown.（改为否定句）

    There _____ a river in _____ hometown.

4. There are some balls in the box.（改为否定句）

    There _____ _____ balls in the box.

Beautiful Nature

UNIT 4

日记导图秀

小朋友，你知道吗？地球上可以饮用的水资源越来越少了，请你模仿上面的日记写一下关于如何节约用水的日记吧！

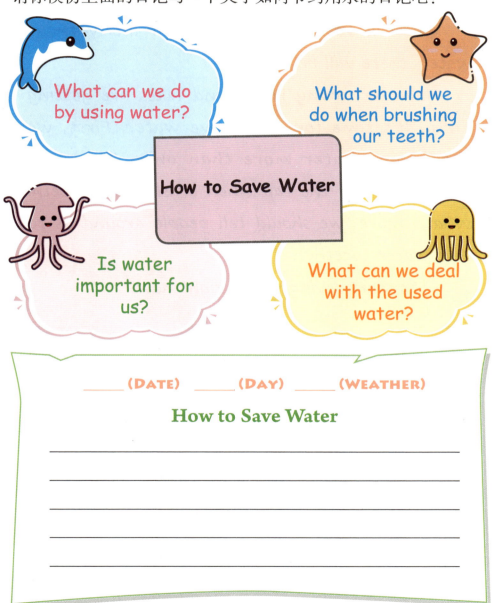

What can we do by using water?

What should we do when brushing our teeth?

How to Save Water

Is water important for us?

What can we deal with the used water?

_____(DATE) _____(DAY) _____(WEATHER)

How to Save Water

_____
_____
_____
_____
_____

参考范文

| December 23rd | Thursday | Cloudy |

How to Save Water

Water is very important in our life. Without water, there will be no life.

However, many rivers and lakes are getting dirty. It's time for us to save water. First, we should use water more than once. Then, we should turn off the tap when brushing our teeth. What's more, we should tell people around us to save water together.

Let's start saving water right now!

词汇加油站

▶ 描述保护环境时还可以用到：

Use the baskets or cloth bags instead of plastic bags. 用篮子或布袋代替塑料袋。

Take the public transportation instead of driving cars. 乘坐公共交通工具而不是开车。

Write down both sides of the paper. 双面使用纸张。

Turn off the lights when leaving the room. 离开房间时关灯。

Unit 5
Future Life and Fantasies

21. My Future House

April 13th   Saturday   Sunny

In the future I will have a big and beautiful house.

The house will be located in the bank of Huangpu River. Every morning when I get up, I will see the beautiful view of Huangpu River. My living room will be very big. There will be a soft sofa and a big TV in the living room. I can sit on the sofa watching TV after I finish my work. In my home, there will be a robot. It can help me do the housework.

What a warm and pretty house!

Unit 5 Future Life and Fantasies

好词妙妙屋

future 将来　　　　　bank 岸边　　　　view 景色
soft 柔软的　　　　　robot 机器人

be located in 坐落在　　　　in the bank of 在岸边
get up 起床　　　　　　　　help sb. do sth. 帮助某人做某事

参考译文

4月13日　　　　星期六　　　　　晴

　　将来我会有一个又大又漂亮的房子。

　　房子会坐落在黄浦江岸边。每天早上起床后，我就能看见黄浦江的美景。我的客厅会非常大，里面有一张柔软的沙发和一台大电视。我完成工作后就会坐在沙发上看电视。我家还会有一个机器人，它会帮我做家务。

　　多么温馨漂亮的一个房子啊！

语法小贴士

　　There be 句型是一个特殊的句子结构，be 动词的单复数形式会根据 be 动词之后的名词来变化。在汉语中，"书桌上有一本书和两支笔。"与"书桌上有两支笔和一本书。"在表达方式上没有区别，但在英语中却不一样。到底有什么不同呢？我们今天就来揭秘吧！

请大家观察以下两个句子：

There is a table and four chairs in the room.

房间里有一张桌子和四把椅子。

There are four chairs and a table in the room.

房间里有四把椅子和一张桌子。

小朋友们，你们发现了吗？这两个句子用的是不同的 be 动词。

在 There be 结构中，be 动词的单复数形式要与 be 动词后边的单词的单复数形式保持一致，也就是我们所说的"就近原则"。

1. 若 be 动词后的名词是单数形式，be 动词用 is；若 be 动词后的名词是复数形式，be 动词用 are。

   There is a cat and two dogs under the tree.

   树底下有一只猫和两只狗。

   There are two dogs and a cat under the tree.

   树底下有两只狗和一只猫。

2. 若 be 动词后的名词是不可数名词，be 动词要用 is。

   There is some water in the glass. 杯子里有一些水。

语法大擂台

读句子，根据句意用 is 或 are 填空。

1. There _____ an apple and two peaches in the plate.
2. There _____ some books and a pencil-box in the bag.
3. There _____ some bread in the basket.
4. _____ there any salt in the bottle?
5. _____ there any students in the classroom?

Unit 5 Future Life and Fantasies

日记导图秀

小朋友，你幻想过自己将来的家是什么样子吗？请你模仿上面的日记描写一下吧！

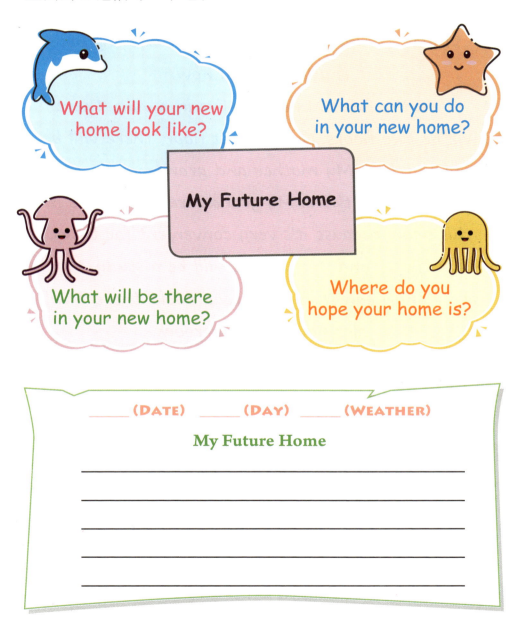

_____ (DATE) _____ (DAY) _____ (WEATHER)

My Future Home

_____

_____

_____

_____

_____

参考范文 🎧 21

September 23rd   Sunday   Sunny

My Future Home

I want to have a new house, because my house is a little small now.

In the future I hope to live in a villa. There will be two floors. On the first floor, there will be a big kitchen. My mother and grandma can cook delicious food there. My grandparents will live in this floor, because it's very convenient for them. On the second floor, there will be a study. My sister and I can study and read books there. I will also have my own room.

词汇加油站

▶ 描写房间还可以用到：

My room faces south. 我的房间朝南。
The bathroom is next to the kitchen.
卫生间在厨房旁边。
I hope my house can be located in the center of the city. 我希望我的家能够位于市中心。
I wish there will be a swimming pool in my home.
我希望我家能拥有一个游泳池。

22. My Future Job

| May 19th | Sunday | Sunny |

In the future, I will be a doctor.

I will work in a hospital and help patients relieve their pain. Sometimes, I will check up the patients and give them some medicine. Sometimes I will do the operation, if the disease is very serious. Every day, I will visit the patients and ask how they feel.

I will be very happy as a doctor, because I will help a lot of people.

我的英语日记书 提高篇

好词妙妙屋

patient 病人　　　　relieve 缓解　　　　pain 疼痛
medicine 药　　　　 disease 疾病　　　　serious 严重的

---

check up 检查　　　　　　　　　　do the operation 做手术
I will be... as... 作为……我会……　a lot of 许多

参考译文

> 5月19日　　　　　　星期日　　　　　　　　晴
>
> 　　将来我会成为一名医生。
> 　　我会在一家医院工作，帮助病人缓解痛苦。有时我会给他们检查身体，并给他们开药。有时，如果他们病情严重的话，我会给他们做手术。每天我都会去看望病人，并且询问他们的病情。
> 　　作为一名医生，我会非常高兴，因为我可以帮助很多人。

语法小贴士

　　小朋友们，你们在写作的时候是不是经常感到无从下笔呢？从今天开始，我们会主要介绍一些在写作中经常用到的句型。小朋友们一定要记清楚了，这样在以后的写作中就不会感到苦恼了。

Unit 5 Future Life and Fantasies

写作常用句型（一）

1. had better do sth. 最好做某事，常用于提建议。

If you want to catch the first bus, you'd better sleep early in the evening. 如果你想赶上首班车，你晚上最好早点睡觉。

2. Thank you/Thanks for doing sth. 谢谢你做某事，常用于表示感谢。

Thank you for helping me with my English. 谢谢你帮我学习英语。

3. not... until... 直到……才……，常用于表达时间。

I didn't sleep until my father came back home. 直到我爸爸回到家我才睡觉。

4. 比较级 + 比较级，越来越……，常用于描述事物的变化。

My hometown becomes more and more beautiful. 我的家乡变得越来越漂亮。

5. ...(not) as (so) + adj./adv. + as... 和……（不）一样，常用于两者之间进行比较。

Our classroom is as big as theirs. 我们的教室和他们的一样大。
Tom runs not so fast as David. 汤姆跑得不如大卫快。

语法大擂台

翻译下列句子。

1. 你睡觉前最好喝一杯牛奶。

_____

2. 谢谢你送了我一本如此有趣的书。

_____

3. 直到我父母回来，我才吃晚饭。

_____

4. 夏天到了，天气越来越热了。

_____

5. 我认为艺术和音乐一样重要。

_____

日记导图秀

小朋友，你幻想过将来的工作吗？请你模仿上面的日记描写一下吧！

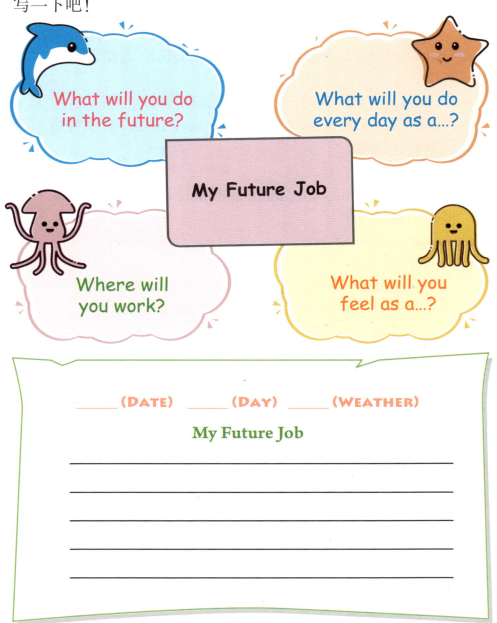

_____ (DATE) _____ (DAY) _____ (WEATHER)

My Future Job

UNIT 5 Future Life and Fantasies

参考范文  22

October 24th　　　　Sunday　　　　Sunny

My Future Job

In the future, I will be the mayor of the city.

As the mayor, I will get up very early every day. I will arrive at the office early. I will read the news and the letters from the citizens. If there are some good suggestions, I will hold a meeting to carry it out. I will visit the old people's home to make sure they are well treated.

词汇加油站

> 描述职业还可以用到：

My job is catching the bad men and protecting the citizens. 我的工作是抓坏人和保护市民。

I take photos for all kinds of people.
我给各行各业的人拍照。

I teach students to learn English at school.
我在学校教学生英语。

23. The Future Cars

March 15th **Friday** **Sunny**

Have you imagined what the future cars will look like?

First, they can change their size. If there is only one person in it, it can be small for only one person. Then they can fly in the sky. If cars fly in the sky, there will not be traffic jams. Besides, they will use the solar energy. This will decrease the pollution. Last, the cars won't need drivers. You just tell it where you want to go, and it can bring you there.

How amazing the future cars are! Do you like them?

UNIT 5
Future Life and Fantasies

好词妙妙屋

imagine 想象　　　　change 改变　　　　size 大小
decrease 减少　　　　pollution 污染

look like 看起来像　　　　traffic jam 交通堵塞
solar energy 太阳能

参考译文

3月15日　　　　星期五　　　　晴

　　你们想象过未来的汽车是什么样子吗？

　　首先，它们可以改变大小。当只有一个乘客时，汽车就只能容纳一个人。它们还可以在空中飞行。如果汽车可以在空中飞行，路上就没有交通堵塞了。此外，汽车将会利用太阳能，这样可以减少污染。最后，汽车不需要司机。你只要告诉汽车想要去的地方，它就会带你去。

　　未来的汽车多么神奇啊！你们喜欢吗？

语法小贴士

写作常用句型（二）

6. **stop... from doing sth. 阻止……做某事，可以用来介绍某物的作用。**

   The trees can stop the wind from blowing away the sand.
   树林可以阻止风吹走沙土。
   I try to stop my father from smoking.
   我努力阻止我爸爸吸烟。

7. **both... and... /either... or... /neither... nor... 两个都/或者……或者……/两个都不，常用于介绍两种事物。**

   Either my mother or my father will take me to the park.
   我妈妈，或者我爸爸将带我去公园。
   Both my father and my mother are doctors.
   我爸爸和妈妈都是医生。

8. **as soon as... 一……就……，常用于表示时间。**

   I will write to you as soon as I arrive in Beijing.
   我一到北京就给您写信。
   It began to rain as soon as I arrived home.
   我一到家就开始下雨了。

9. **so + *adj./adv.* that... 如此……以至于……，常用于引出结果。**

Future Life and Fantasies

UNIT 5

He ran so fast that he got the first place.

他跑得如此快，以至于得了第一名。

She is so polite that everyone likes her.

她如此懂礼貌，以至于所有人都喜欢她。

10. though + 句子，尽管……，常用于表示让步关系。

Though I was very tired, I felt very happy.

尽管我今天很累，但是我很高兴。

语法大擂台

翻译下列句子。

1. 植物可以阻止土壤被水冲走。

   _____

2. 我和我哥哥都还没有毕业。

   _____

3. 我回到家就开始写作业。

   _____

4. 我作业做得不认真，结果做错了一些。

   _____

5. 尽管天气很冷，但我们心里感到很温暖。

   _____

日记导图秀

小朋友，你幻想过未来的学校是什么样吗？请你模仿上面的日记描写一下吧！

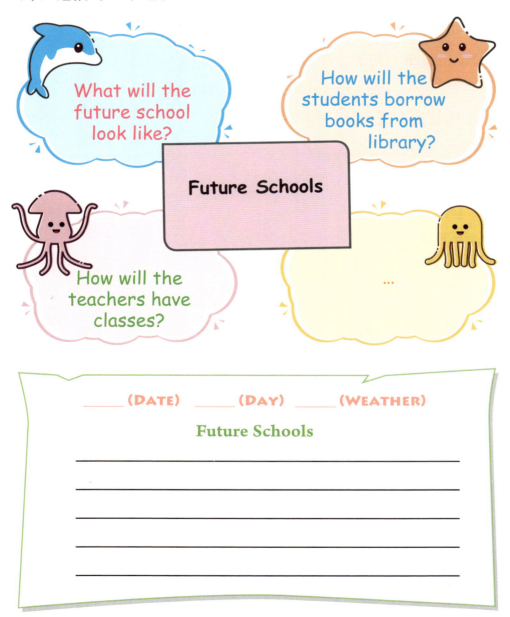

UNIT 5 Future Life and Fantasies

参考范文

April 26th   Friday   Sunny

Future Schools

In the future, schools will be different. They will be under the sea, on the mountain, and even in space.

Teachers can have classes at home. They can have classes through the computer. There will be robots at school. They can help students clean the classroom. In the library, if students want to borrow some books, they can just input the names of the books in the computer, and then the robot will bring the books to them.

词汇加油站

> 描写未来的事物还可能用到：

In the future, we can live in space.
未来我们可以在太空居住。

In the future, any disease can be cured.
未来任何疾病都能够被治愈。

There will be less pollution in the future.
在未来，污染会变少。

24. If I Had the Wings

December 24th   **Tuesday**   **Sunny**

I always imagine how nice if I had the wings. I would be very free, and I could fly to wherever I want to go. I would fly back to Australia to meet my friends and visit the Sydney Opera House. I would also fly to Tibet to visit the Potala Palace. It must be very great. If I had the wings, I would fly to some poor areas to help the children. I would teach them English.

UNIT 5 Future Life and Fantasies

好词妙妙屋

wing 翅膀　　　　free 自由的　　　　poor 贫穷的

fly back to 飞回　　　　　the Potala Palace 布达拉宫

参考译文

12月24日　　　　　星期二　　　　　晴

　　我总是幻想，要是我有一双翅膀该多好啊！我会非常自由，而且我可以飞到任何我想去的地方。我会飞回澳大利亚去找我的朋友玩。我们会去悉尼歌剧院。我也想飞去西藏，去参观布达拉宫。它肯定非常壮观。如果我有一双翅膀，我会飞到贫困的地方去帮助那些孩子们。我会教他们英语。

语法小贴士

写作常用句型（三）

11. be different from 与……不同，常用于表示两事物的不同或同一事物在不同时间段的不同。

Now, my hometown is different from what it used to be.
现在，我的家乡和以前不一样了。

Their school is different from ours.
他们的学校与我们的不同。

12. **have no time to do sth.** 没有时间做某事。描述某人很忙的时候可以用这个句型。

    I am usually very busy on weekdays, so I have no time to watch TV. 我通常在工作日很忙，因此我没有时间看电视。

13. **used to** 过去常常，用于描述过去的事情。

    My father used to smoke. 我爸爸过去经常抽烟。
    When I was young, I used to swim in the river.
    我小时候常常去河里游泳。

14. **be famous for** 因……而著名，常用于描述一个人或地方因为某事而闻名。

    Hangzhou is famous for the West Lake. 杭州因西湖而闻名。

15. **it is said that** 据说……，用于描述某个地点和某事。

    It is said that this building is the oldest in the city.
    据说这是这个城市最古老的建筑。

语法大擂台

翻译下列句子。

1. Lucy 的书包不同于 Lily 的。

   _____

2. 我没有时间锻炼。

   _____

Future Life and Fantasies

UNIT 5

3. 我过去常常在小河里游泳。
   _____

4. 北京因长城而闻名。
   _____

5. 据说火星上有人居住。
   _____

日记导图秀

小朋友，你幻想过什么吗？请你模仿上面的日记描写一下吧！

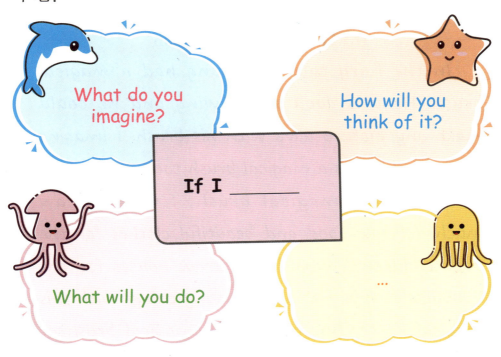

_____ (Date) _____ (Day) _____ (Weather)

If I _____

February 4th   Friday   Sunny

If I Had a Magical Brush

In the fairy tale, Ma Liang had a magical brush. He was good at drawing and he could make any picture alive with his brush. I imagine that I could have a magical brush too!

If I had a magical brush, I would draw much delicious food and beautiful clothes for the poor children. I would also draw houses for the homeless people. I would do many things with this magical brush. But there is no magical brush at all. If I want to help others, I must work hard.

Unit 5 Future Life and Fantasies

词汇加油站

> 描写幻想时还可能用到：

if I could fly 如果我可以飞

if there was a robot in my home 如果我家有一个机器人

if I had one million dollars 如果我有 100 万美元

if I were given three wishes 如果给我三个愿望

I wish I could be a superman. 我希望我是一个超人。

25. I Had a Dream

July 21st　　　　　**Sunday**　　　　　**Rainy**

Yesterday night, I had a dream. In my dream, I turned to be a superman.

I flew to the poor mountains and brought the children books and computers. They were very happy. I went to help the firefighters put out the big fire and save people trapped in the fire. I was very proud of myself.

I was awoken by the alarm. I would study hard to help more people.

UNIT 5 Future Life and Fantasies

好词妙妙屋

turn 变成　　superman 超人　　mountain 山
firefighter 消防员　trapped 被困的　awake 唤醒

put out 熄灭　　　　　　be proud of... 为……感到自豪

参考译文

7月21日　　　　星期日　　　　　　雨

昨天晚上我做了一个梦，我梦见自己变成了超人。

我飞到了贫困的山区，给孩子们带去了书本和电脑。孩子们非常高兴。我还帮助消防员灭火、营救被困在大火中的人。我为自己感到非常自豪。

我是被闹铃叫醒的。我要努力学习，去帮助更多的人。

语法小贴士

写作常用句型（四）

16. with one's help = with the help of 在某人的帮助下，常用于介绍别人的帮忙。

    With your help/With the help of you, I finished my homework. 在你的帮助下，我完成了作业。

17. It's time to do sth. 该去做……了，常用于说明某时间该做的事。

    It's 7:00. It's time to get up. 7点了，该起床了。

18. **I (don't) think** 我（不）认为，常用于陈述某个观点。

    I think it is good to take exercises every morning.
    我认为每天早上锻炼非常好。

19. **prefer to do... rather than do...** 宁愿做……也不愿做……，常用于做选择。

    In the past, I preferred to stay at home rather than go camping. 我以前宁愿待在家里也不愿去宿营。

20. **表示"花钱"的句型：**

    sb. spend + 时间 / 金钱 (in) doing sth. / on sth.

    It takes sb. + 时间 to do sth.

    sb. pays + 金钱 for sth.

    I spent five dollars in buying this ball.

    我花了 5 美元买的这个球。

    It took me 30 minutes to finish the housework.

    我花了 30 分钟才做完家务。

    I paid 50 dollars for this dress.

    我花了 50 美元买的这条裙子。

语法大擂台

翻译下列句子。

1. 在老师的帮助下，我通过了考试。

   _____

2. 据说我们下学期将有一位新的英语老师。

   _____

Unit 5 Future Life and Fantasies

3. 我认为不会下雨。
   _____

4. 这么热的天，我宁愿待在家里也不愿去游泳。
   _____

5. 这位作家花了三年的时间才写完这本小说。
   _____

日记导图秀

小朋友，你做过梦吗？梦里都发生了什么？请你模仿上面的日记描写一下吧！

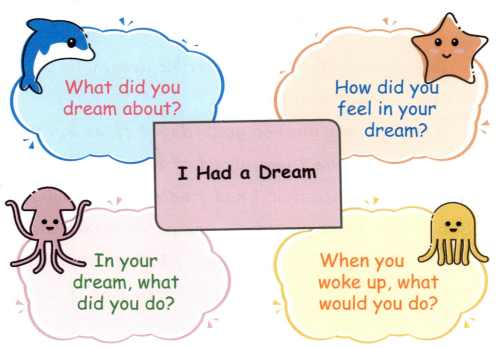

_____ (Date) _____ (Day) _____ (Weather)

I Had a Dream

June 24th   **Saturday**   **Sunny**

I Had a Dream

Yesterday night I had a terrible dream. In the dream, I had a very long nose.

I lied to my mother yesterday. I came home very late. Because I was afraid of being punished, I told my mother that I had studied with Dobby. But in fact, I just played the computer games and forgot the time. And at night, I had a dream. I dreamed my nose turned to be very long. I was woken up by the nightmare.

What a terrible dream! I would never tell lies.

Unit 5 Future Life and Fantasies

词汇加油站

▶ 描写做梦还可能用到：

I dreamed about failing the exam. 我梦见考试不及格。

I dreamed about a friend of mine in my hometown.
我梦见了我家乡的一个朋友。

In my dream, I met my idol, Beckham.
在梦里，我见到了我的偶像——贝克汉姆。

参考答案

Unit 1   About Me

1 Myself
语法大擂台
1. get up
2. supermarket
3. taking a photo
4. drew
5. is cooking
6. football
7. visit
8. go to bed

2 My Parents
语法大擂台
1. drinks
2. goes
3. stays
4. makes
5. looks
6. passes
7. carries
8. comes
9. plants
10. brushes
11. does
12. has

3 My Dream
语法大擂台
1. buy
2. play
3. works
4. speak
5. Do; go
6. Does; like

4 My Favorite Season
语法大擂台
1. Dobby and Amy are watering the grapes.
2. Fangfang is swimming in the pool.
3. We are having a picnic in the park.
4. A boy is playing football under a tree.
5. Dobby and his friend are planting trees.

5 I Have a Computer

语法大擂台

1. lived　　　2. watched　　　3. opened
4. studied　　5. loved　　　　6. tried
7. cried　　　8. stopped　　　9. planned

Unit 2　Travel and Places

6 Travel Plan

语法大擂台

1. swam; C　　　　2. sang; D
3. ate; A　　　　　4. flew; E
5. fell; B　　　　　6. drank; H
7. ran; I　　　　　8. rode; J
9. swept; F　　　　10. drew; G

7 The Great Wall

语法大擂台

1. rode a bike　　　2. swept
3. got up　　　　　4. planted
5. swam　　　　　　6. visited
7. took part in　　　8. went

8 My Hometown

语法大擂台

I. 1. will; B　2. Are; going to; C　3. will; D　4. Will; A

II. 1. is going to visit; next month

　　isn't going to visit; next month

　　Is your father going to visit; next month

2. will learn to swim
   won't learn to swim
   Will; learn to swim

9 My School
语法大擂台

1. will/am going to
2. will/is going to be
3. will/is going to work
4. will/are going to have

10 Visiting Mount Tai
语法大擂台

I. 1. running; C   2. eating; F   3. closing; E
    4. crying; B   5. lying; D   6. raining; A

II. 1. is raining   2. is skipping
    3. are making a snowman   4. is drawing

Unit 3　A Colorful Life

11 A Day in the Zoo
语法大擂台

1. singing
2. skating
3. eating a banana
4. taking a bath
5. having a meal

12 My Birthday Party
语法大擂台

1. go to school
2. There are
3. I will go to
4. bought; a new skirt
5. asks; to tidy up

13 On Duty

语法大擂台

1. Do you
2. didn't make
3. can't play
4. Can Tom run
5. Will you go

14 Sports Meeting

语法大擂台

一般疑问句：A, E

特殊疑问句：C, F

选择疑问句：B, D

15 My First Day at School

语法大擂台

1. Yes, I am.
2. No, I'm not.
3. Yes, I do.
4. No, I won't.

Unit 4　Beautiful Nature

16 The River in My Hometown

语法大擂台

Where　When　How　What　Which　Why

17 My Favorite Animal

语法大擂台

1. nurse　2. guitar　3. the Great Wall　4. Math　5. By bike

18 Winter Is Coming!

语法大擂台

1—C　2—D　3—E　4—A　5—B

⑲ A Clever Crow
语法大擂台

1. What 2. How 3. How 4. What 5. What

⑳ How to Protect the Environment
语法大擂台

1. Is there; your; Yes, there is

2. Are there any; No, there aren't

3. isn't; my

4. aren't any

Unit 5　Future Life and Fantasies

㉑ My Future House
语法大擂台

1. is 2. are 3. is 4. Is 5. Are

㉒ My Future Job
语法大擂台

1. You'd better drink a glass of milk before going to bed.

2. Thanks for giving me such an interesting book.

3. I didn't have dinner until my parents came back.

4. Summer is coming, and it becomes hotter and hotter.

5. I think art is as important as music.

㉓ The Future Cars
语法大擂台

1. Plants can stop the soil from being rushed away by water.

2. Neither I nor my brother has graduated from school.

3. I began to do my homework as soon as I arrived home.

4. I wrote my homework so carelessly that I made some mistakes.

5. Though it is very cold, we felt very warm from the heart.

24 If I Had the Wings

语法大擂台

1. Lucy's bag is different from Lily's.

2. I have no time to do exercises.

3. I used to swim in the river.

4. Beijing is famous for the Great Wall.

5. It's said that there are people living on the Mars.

25 I Had a Dream

语法大擂台

1. With the teacher's help, I passed the exam. /

   With the help of the teacher, I passed the exam.

2. It's said that there will be a new English teacher next term.

3. I don't think it's going to rain.

4. I prefer to stay at home rather than swim in such a hot day.

5. It took the writer three years to finish this novel. /

   The writer spent three years in finishing this novel.